KU-535-078

soup

RYLAND
PETERS
& SMALL

LONDON NEW YORK

elsa petersen-schepelern

photography by **peter cassidy**

soup

Dedicated to
Kirsten Bray and Mabs Docherty

Production Patricia Harrington
Art Director Gabriella Le Grazie
Publishing Director Alison Starling

Food Stylist Linda Tubby
Prop Stylists Helen Trent and Róisín Nield
Indexer Hilary Bird

Published in the United Kingdom in 2003
by Ryland Peters & Small
Kirkman House, 12–14 Whitfield Street
London W1T 2RP
www.rylandpeters.com

10 9 8 7 6 5 4 3 2 1

Text © Elsa Petersen-Schepelern 2003
Design and photographs
© Ryland Peters & Small 2003

The author's moral rights have been asserted.
All rights reserved. No part of this publication
may be reproduced, stored in a retrieval
system or transmitted in any form or by
any means, electronic, mechanical,
photocopying or otherwise, without the prior
permission of the publisher.

ISBN 1 84172 493 9

A catalogue record for this book is available
from the British Library.

Printed and bound in China.

Notes

All spoon measurements are level.

All eggs are large, unless otherwise specified.
Uncooked or partly cooked eggs should not
be served to the very young, the very old,
those with compromised immune systems,
or to pregnant women.

Author's Acknowledgements

As usual, I would like to thank Pete Cassidy
and Linda Tubby for their beautiful work.
Thanks also to my sister Kirsten and nephews
Peter Bray and Luc Votan, and to Susan,
Martin, Tessa, Karen and Mike, who have
tasted their way through the testing. Friends
and fellow food writers have also been
generous with their time and advice – Clare
Ferguson, Sonia Stevenson, Alastair Hendy,
Shona Adhikari, Praveen Anand and Linda
Tubby among others. My grateful thanks also
to my editors, Susan Stuck and Roy Butcher –
plus designer Paul Tilby, who is far too inclined
to hide his light under a bushel.

contents

sup a soup for supper . . .

Soup is one of those instantly satisfying, all-purpose dishes that fits into almost any occasion. Serve it as a first course for lunch or dinner, or as a satisfying whole-meal dish. In this book, I've explained some of the basics of soup making, so that you can use these methods to create your own recipes from your favourite ingredients, or whatever you find fresh on the day.

Start with stocks. Like most people, I don't have time to make my own, except for a special occasion, but I've found good sources of fresh stock instead. My local butcher makes it and some supermarkets sell fresh stock in tubs. Once, stock cubes were very much frowned upon, but if you find a good brand – one that's not too salty – by all means use it. In any case, drying food for transport or for use in the winter is one of those ancient skills that makes us human. Use it!

Try the recipes for Asian stocks – dashi, Chinese and several South-east Asian. I always have some dashi stock powder on hand, though it's a matter of moments to make it from scratch and all the ingredients are dried. The only stocks I usually make myself are South-east Asian – incredibly delicious and fragrant and worth every second of preparation time.

I've also given a basic outline of how to make cream soups. Don't think they always contain cream – the word refers to the fact that they are blended or puréed into a cream. Whatever kind you'd like to make, it always begins with gently frying onions and other flavouring vegetables. Then you add more vegetables, flavourings, stock or water – followed by a final visit to some sort of blending machine. When you understand the framework, you can repeat it with

soup for supper

In medieval times, in most of the peasant houses in Europe, especially northern Europe, soup or stew was almost the only dish. Nobody had a domestic oven, and in any case, they couldn't afford the large amount of fuel needed to cook roast meats. A fire in the hearth kept people warm and heated the contents of a cauldron suspended over the top. A large tureen of soup was served in the middle of the table, then ladled out into bowls and eaten with bread. At first, the bread – known as the 'sop' – was put in the bowl, then the soup poured over it (and of course became sopping wet). It's also how we got the word 'supper'— a cosy family meal without pretensions. Soup of course.

Gradually, soup lost its place as the only kind of meal, and became a first course, as well as keeping its place as the main course in a light, informal lunch or family supper.

In other parts of the world, soup forms a different function. In Vietnam, it's breakfast in the form of the famous pho – a dish that seems to me to be nutritionally complete. It contains noodles for carbohydrate, beef or chicken for protein, vegetables and mountains of fresh herbs for essential vitamins and minerals, plus nutritious stock that fills the belly and slakes the thirst. Add a squeeze of lime for vitamin C, and there we are. In China, Korea, Japan and many parts of South-east Asia, soup appears at almost every meal – the sipping liquid instead of the water or wine that we might use.

many other ingredients, not just the examples in the recipes I have given. All the other soups progress in much the same way, but I've given an outline on pages 96–97 of how to prepare most kinds of pasta, rice and noodles, so you can add them to a soup – they take only minutes to cook.

I have a passion for pulses of all sorts, in soups, stews, salads and other vegetable dishes. Peas and lentils don't have to be soaked, but beans do, so on pages 74–75, I've given you a quick reference so you'll know how long to soak and cook most popular dried beans. But frankly – like everyone – I'm very happy to use the canned kind. Canning and bottling is a time-honoured kitchen tradition, so let's not get snobbish about it because it's cheap and easy to use them this way.

a question of etiquette

All countries have their own collection of table etiquette, based on historical, religious and social backgrounds. My mother always said that good manners are simply the most efficient way of doing things. But it didn't stop her being a stickler for form. 'Don't put your napkin on the table.' 'Don't slurp your soup!' she said, as nicely brought up mothers always do. Of course, if she were Japanese, or Vietnamese, or from anywhere east of Suez, slurping her soup would have been the height of good manners. If you didn't, people would think you weren't enjoying it. But in our house, a girl slurping her soup would result in a table full of raised adult eyebrows and a glance to my mother, which clearly said, 'Well, really!' 'Do something!'

It also depends on where you grew up. If you're British or American, you would be taught to sip your soup from the side of the spoon, and to tip the plate away from you. If you were French, you'd be told on no account to tip the plate. In Japan, you'd sip the liquid from your soup from an elegant lidded lacquer bowl, holding it by the foot and rim so you wouldn't burn yourself, then you'd eat the rest with chopsticks (the pointed Japanese kind).

a spoon to sup a soup with

In the West, the evolution of the soup spoon has been through shades of etiquette that most of us have forgotten about. We think that a round bowled spoon that doesn't hold very much is a soup spoon. It's not. It's a Victorian invention, so each hostess could outdo the next in the complexity of her silver. Elegant Victorians used a tablespoon (opposite below) for soup, unless it was a cream soup, when they would use a spoon with a big round bowl (opposite above), or a bouillon (a clear soup) which was sipped from a spoon which had a slightly smaller bowl. But you had to be careful with consommés, because the spoon was there only to test the heat of the soup – then you picked up the bowl by its handles and sipped (politely of course).

Then, in the 1950s, America started to make cutlery sets with dessert spoons, bouillon spoons – and only two soup (table) spoons, which were supposed to be used for serving. Soon, everyone was at it, and some of the finest designers in the world made spoons that were incredibly elegant, but so flat they could hold no soup! Beautiful but utterly impractical.

Though proper soup spoons are still made by some sensible manufacturers, I find the best and cheapest places to buy them is at antique markets – one of the most enjoyable places to shop anyway.

stocks

beef stock and brown stock

Though fresh stocks are often available in larger supermarkets, and most people will admit to using stock cubes or powders from time to time, homemade stocks are infinitely better. Beef stocks in particular are worth making yourself. Use them in soups, long-cooked traditional stews and to reduce into sauces.

2 kg beef bones

3 tablespoons unsalted butter or oil (not olive oil) or a mixture of both

500 g stewing beef, cut into 2 cm cubes

2 large onions, chopped

2 large carrots, chopped

a small handful of parsley, stalks bruised

1 tablespoon black peppercorns, lightly crushed

1 leek, split in 4 lengthways and well washed, then coarsely chopped

2 celery stalks, finely sliced

1 bouquet garni (a bunch of herbs tied up with kitchen string)

makes about 2 litres

Note I add a halved tomato and sometimes a small piece of liver to the stock at the same time as the herbs. I find they make the stock clearer and more flavourful.

To make basic beef stock, put all the ingredients in a large stockpot, cover with 4 litres water and bring to the boil. Reduce the heat to a simmer. For the first 30 minutes, you must skim off the foam that rises to the surface. This will help make the stock clearer and less fatty. It should be just hot enough to let a large, slow bubble break on the surface of the liquid. Do not let it boil, or the fat will be constantly redistributed through the stock.

When cooking is complete, remove from the heat and strain through a colander into a large bowl. Discard the solids. Let the stock cool, then transfer to the refrigerator, cover and chill overnight. Next morning, scrape off the fat that will have risen to the top.

Strain through a fine sieve, then ladle into conveniently sized containers: 1 litre will serve 4 people.

If you are left with a little stock that's not enough for a whole recipe, pour it into ice cube trays, freeze, then keep in freezer bags – whenever you need 'a tablespoon of stock', the cube equals about a tablespoon.

To make brown stock, put the bones in a roasting tin and roast in a preheated oven at 200°C (400°F) Gas 6 for about 30 minutes or until browned.

Meanwhile, heat the butter or butter and oil in a large stockpot, add the beef cubes, without crowding the pan (in batches if necessary), and fry until browned on all sides.

Add the onions and carrots and sauté until browned. The success of the stock depends on good browning of the meat, bones, onions and carrots. The caramelized sugars give colour and flavour, but take care not to burn.

Add the browned beef bones, the parsley, peppercorns, leek, celery and bouquet garni. Bring to the boil, then reduce the heat and simmer, covered, for at least 4 hours.

Note Beef bones don't contain enough gelatine to make a jellied stock. To achieve a jelly, include a few veal bones or chicken carcasses. Traditionally, a split pig's trotter would be included, though these are becoming more and more difficult to find.

lamb, ham or pork stock

Don't include lamb or pork bones in a basic brown stock – they will make it very sweet. If you wish to make a lamb or pork stock, you must take even more care to remove fat at every stage. Lamb stocks are used in Middle Eastern and North African cooking; pork stock mostly in Asian cooking, but often in combination with chicken; ham stock is traditional with peas.

veal stock

This is the famous white stock of *haute cuisine* fame. Veal stock is delicious, and I used to make it often when I lived in Australia, where veal was raised humanely. Now I live in Europe, where the issue of animal welfare for pork and veal is very important. Ask for organically raised meat if you want to make this stock. The meat itself is expensive, so halve the quantities given for beef stock.

Follow the recipe for beef stock, substituting veal bones for beef bones and stewing veal for stewing beef. The meat and bones may be browned or not (if not, then it's called white stock). As with lamb stock, you should pay particular attention to skimming and defatting. This stock is very gelatinous and excellent for making sauces.

chicken stock

Chicken stock was traditionally made using an old boiling fowl, full of flavour. These are almost impossible to find these days, and the next best things are, in my opinion, kosher chickens, chicken carcasses, chicken wings or drumsticks.

2 kg chicken carcasses, a whole chicken, or pieces as above	2 tablespoons peppercorns, lightly crushed
2 onions, chopped	1 fresh bay leaf, or ½ dried
2 carrots, chopped	1 leek, split in 4 lengthways, well washed, then chopped
1 celery stalk, chopped	
a few sprigs of parsley, stalks bruised	**makes 2 litres**

Put all the ingredients in a large stockpot, add 3 litres cold water and bring to the boil. As the water heats, skim off the foam from time to time. Reduce to simmering and cook, uncovered, for at least 4 hours. Skim off the foam as it accumulates.

Strain through a colander into a bowl, let cool, then chill overnight. Next day, scrape off the fat that has risen to the top. Decant into 1 litre containers, then freeze. When frozen, Sonia Stevenson then splashes boiling water over the surface to rinse off the last few drops of fat – a trick she learned from a Chinese chef.

fish stock

Though most fishmongers will sell you fish frames and heads, you can also save them and freeze them from normal household fish cooking until you have enough for stock. Do not use any oily fish, such as mackerel, tuna, bonito, salmon or trout. The rule with all fish stocks is that you mustn't let the bones boil for more than 30 seconds or they will make the stock gluey. After straining, don't let it stay at boiling or simmering point for more than 30 minutes.

2 kg heads and frames of white fish	1 small celery stalk, very finely chopped	1 small leek, split lengthways, well washed, then very finely chopped
75 g unsalted butter	a few sprigs of parsley, stalks bruised, then finely chopped	150 ml white wine
2 onions, very finely chopped		
1 carrot, very finely chopped	1 teaspoon peppercorns	**makes 1 litre**

First, trim the gills out of the fish heads (or get the fishmonger to do it for you). These make stock bitter.

Melt the butter in a large saucepan or stockpot, then add the onions, carrot, celery, parsley, peppercorns and leek and cook gently until softened and translucent. Don't let it brown. Add the wine and bring to the boil, then add 1 litre iced water and ice cubes. The butter will stick to the ice cubes and you can remove them. Add the fish heads and frames, bring to the boil again, reduce the heat and simmer for 30 minutes, skimming occasionally. Remove from the heat and strain out the solids. Strain again through a fine sieve.

Return the strained stock to the rinsed-out saucepan and return to the boil. Simmer until reduced by about a third or a half, to intensify the flavour. Use immediately, or let cool, then chill. When cold, decant into small containers, about 250–500 ml.

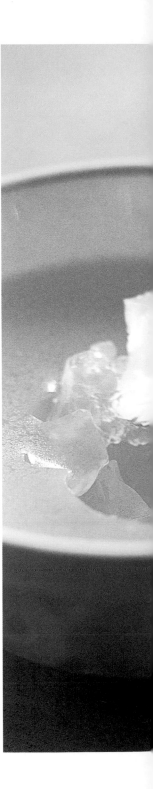

vegetable stock

To produce delicious caramelized tastes, roast the vegetables before using in stock. Go lightly on highly flavoured items like celery or fennel. I also omit floury vegetables like potatoes, and any member of the cabbage family, which is inclined to develop sour tastes.

2 garlic cloves, crushed

1 large onion, chopped

3 large leeks, halved, washed well and chopped

2 large carrots, chopped

2 celery stalks, chopped

a handful of parsley stalks, lightly crushed

2 bay leaves

a sprig of thyme

40 g unsalted butter, melted

1 tablespoon olive oil

250 ml white wine

makes 1 litre

Put all the vegetables in a plastic bag, then add the butter and oil and shake the bag so everything is equally covered in oil. Transfer to a roasting tin and extract every last drop of oil from the bag. Roast the vegetables in a preheated oven at 200°C (400°F) Gas 6 for 40–45 minutes, turning them from time to time. Transfer the vegetables to a stockpot and put the empty tin on top of the stove. Add the wine and 500 ml water and scrape up any residues from the tin. Pour into the stockpot.

Add 2½ litres cold water and bring to the boil. Reduce the heat, cover with a lid and let simmer for 1 hour. Remove from the heat and let cool.

Strain the stock through a fine sieve and discard the vegetables and flavourings. Pour the stock back into the rinsed pan and bring to the boil. Keep boiling until reduced by half. Use immediately or let cool and use within 2 days or freeze.

microwave stocks

3 crushed parsley stalks

1 onion, chopped

1 carrot, chopped

1 celery stalk, chopped,

500 g chicken pieces such as wings, or meat bones and trimmings

makes about 500 ml

Put all the ingredients in a lidded microwave bowl, fill almost to the top with boiling water and microwave on HIGH for 35 minutes. Let stand for 30 minutes, then strain off the liquid and discard the solids. Cool at room temperature until the fat rises to the surface, then chill.

Remove and discard the fat, then use the stock within 1–2 days or freeze. (Strain through muslin for a clearer stock.)

For vegetable stocks, omit the chicken, add extra vegetables and microwave on HIGH for 20 minutes, then let stand for 20 minutes.

asian stocks

Most Asian cuisines are well populated with soups. Some take the place of water to be sipped throughout the meal. Others are the bases of whole-meal soups, such as pho bo or Japanese New Year soup.

If you go to Asian supermarkets, you will see soup and stock bases in powder or liquid form for almost every soup you can think of. Dashi stocks are quick and convenient in this form, as are miso, Thai tom yam and Vietnamese pho. There are many brands. If you find one you like, stick to it – or make your own from one of the recipes here.

Check the packet for any mention of the dreaded MSG or 'taste powder' – a perfectly legitimate Asian ingredient, but one to which foreigners have taken a definite dislike. Whether it tastes peculiar, or makes you high or not, it is, after all, a form of salt, and most of us would like to add salt only to our own taste.

chinese stock

Chinese stocks are as varied as those of any other country, but often use chicken and meat together – usually pork. This one is a good base for all sorts of soups. Traditionally, people drink soup with a Chinese meal, and they sip it throughout, between mouthfuls of other foods. China is a huge country, with many regional cuisines – a whole book could be written on the soups of China, so the ones found here are just a taste.

500 g chicken carcass, bones or wings

500 g meaty pork bones, such as ribs

a chunk of fresh ginger, sliced

6 spring onions, halved lengthways

makes 1 litre

Put the chicken and pork in a large saucepan, add the ginger and spring onions and cover with about 2 litres cold water. Bring slowly to the boil, reduce the heat and simmer for 2–3 hours. Skim off the foam from time to time, especially at the beginning. The stock should be clear, so don't let it boil. When cooked, ladle off the soup into a separate pan – disturbing the sediment will cloud the stock. Use immediately or let cool, then refrigerate. The fat will rise to the surface and become almost solid (chicken fat on its own does not solidify, but the pork will help it do so).

To serve soup during a meal, reheat the stock, then add other ingredients to taste – just a few, perhaps not more than three. Suggestions include chopped spring onions, corn, shredded cooked chicken, a little sliced meat, crab meat, egg, beancurd (tofu), green vegetables such as shredded spinach, or mushrooms.

Variations You can also make this stock with all chicken or all pork.

japanese dashi stocks

Many Japanese dishes, not just soups, use one of several kinds of basic stock, or dashi. The first recipe is a clear stock used for clear soups, the others are also used in other dishes. Bonito is a kind of small tuna, which is dried then grated so the flavour will more easily disperse. Though you can buy dashi stock powders to be reconstituted with water, it's not complicated to make it yourself. The dried base ingredients are easily stored.

first dashi

1 sheet kombu, about 20 cm long
500 ml dried shaved bonito

makes about 1¼ litres

Using a damp cloth, wipe the kombu, but leave the white powder, which has wonderful flavour. Slit the kombu in several places. Put it in a saucepan and add 1¼ litres water. Set aside for 1 hour to soak.

Bring slowly to the boil over medium heat, but remove the kombu just before the water boils – otherwise the stock will smell too seaweedy.

Lower the heat and sprinkle in the shaved bonito.

Let boil for about 1 minute and skim off the foam with a slotted spoon. Remove from the heat and set aside.

Let the bonito settle to the bottom, then carefully strain through a muslin-lined sieve into a bowl.

Reserve the kombu and bonito shavings from this dashi to make the second.

second dashi

Put the kombu from the First Dashi in a saucepan. Add the reserved bonito from the muslin, then 1 litre water. Bring to the boil and again remove the kombu just before boiling point.

Continue boiling for about 4 minutes, then strain through muslin into a second bowl.

south-east asian stocks

thai stock

This simple stock can be made with all chicken or chicken and pork. Use it as a basis for soups and curries.

1½ kg chicken carcasses, chopped into 4–6 pieces, or wings

500 g lean pork with bones, cut in large chunks

a handful of coriander with stalks and roots if possible

a large pinch of salt

makes 1 litre

Put the chicken, pork and coriander in a large saucepan, add a large pinch of salt and about 2 litres water. Bring to the boil and skim off any foam that rises to the surface. Repeat the skimming several times, then reduce the heat to a gentle simmer and cook for about 1 hour.

Remove from the heat and let cool. When cool, ladle gently through a fine strainer so as not to disturb too much of the sediment. Discard the bones and sediment.

Chill for several hours or overnight, then scrape off the fat from the top of the stock. Use immediately, or freeze in convenient quantities.

vietnamese chicken or pork stock

A basic stock made from any available poultry or meat. When the stock is strained, reserve any small pieces of meat or chicken and use them in salads. The sugar/salt/spice combination is very common in Vietnam.

2 kg chicken carcasses, pork bones, or a combination

3 cm fresh ginger, thickly sliced

1 shallot or onion, cut into wedges

a pinch of salt

a pinch of sugar

makes 1 litre

Put the bones in a large saucepan and cover completely with cold water. Bring slowly to the boil and boil for 10–15 minutes, skimming off the foam several times.

Reduce the heat, add the ginger, shallot or onion, salt and sugar, then simmer for about 2 hours.

Pour carefully through a fine strainer, discarding the bones, flavourings and sediment. Use the stock immediately, or freeze.

vietnamese beef stock

The basis of the legendary Vietnamese beef noodle soup, Pho Bo, and of many other soups, this beef stock is very useful. In Vietnam, it is made only by the pho vendors because ordinary kitchens don't have the space or fuel to deal with huge pots and hours of cooking. Take advantage of Western kitchen technology with its big stoves and freezers – cook in quantity, freeze it in 500 ml containers and use as required.

1 kg shin of beef, with bones, cut in 3 cm slices

500 g stewing beef, in the piece

a chunk of fresh ginger, peeled and sliced

a pinch of salt

3 tablespoons fish sauce

2 whole star anise

1 cinnamon stick, broken

2 onions, sliced

makes about 3 litres

Put the bones in a large saucepan, cover completely with cold water, at least 3 litres, and bring to the boil. Boil for about 15 minutes, skimming the foam off the top every few minutes. When the foam stops rising, reduce the heat, add the stewing beef and simmer for about 2 hours.

Add the ginger, salt, fish sauce, star anise, cinnamon stick and onions and continue simmering for about 30 minutes.

Carefully pour through a fine sieve, then discard the bones, flavourings and sediment. Reserve the meat for another dish.

Use the stock within 3 days or freeze in 500 ml containers.

south-east asian chicken stock

This is one of the most delicious chicken stocks I've ever tasted. Make it with a free-range, organic or kosher chicken, then eat the chicken later shredded into salads, or in chicken soups.

1 small free-range chicken

2 whole star anise

2 cinnamon sticks

4 kaffir lime leaves

2 stalks of lemongrass, halved lengthways and bruised

a large chunk of ginger, peeled and cut in slices

4 garlic cloves, crushed but whole

1 red chilli, halved lengthways

1 tablespoon peppercorns, bruised

makes about 1 litre

Put the chicken, breast up, in a saucepan or casserole dish of about 1½ litre capacity. Add the star anise, cinnamon, kaffir lime leaves, lemongrass, ginger, garlic, chilli and peppercorns, then add water to cover by 3 cm. If the chicken starts to float, tip it up so that any air trapped in the cavity is released. Also, I sometimes put a small saucer on the bird to hold it down. Bring the water to the boil, reduce the heat and simmer for at least 1 hour, turning the bird after about 30 minutes.

Remove the chicken, whole, from the pan and reserve to use in another dish.

Strain the stock into a pan, ladling at first, then pouring through muslin. It should be clear but fatty on top. The fat is not a problem for Asians, but Europeans may like to blot it off. Alternatively, use chef Sonia Stevenson's freezing and defatting method at the end of the Chicken Stock recipe on page 14. Taste the stock for flavour. If not intense enough, reduce it by boiling down to about half volume. Use immediately, or cool and chill or freeze in conveniently sized containers.

clear soups

clarifying stock

1 litre beef, chicken or fish stock

125 g beef, chicken or fish,
well trimmed of fat

3 egg whites

crushed shells of 2 eggs

Consommé and its chilled cousin, jellied consommé, were once the very epitome of the soup-maker's art. They still are, if less common these days. Clarifying can be a little time-consuming, but what's that to a keen cook? For your entertainment, here's how to do it.

General framework for clarifying stock

• First, you must take care to produce a clear stock from the beginning, because if you let it become fatty, it can't be clarified. When you make the stock (pages 10–19), do so without emulsifying it. That means don't let the stock boil so that the fat is combined with the other liquids. It should then be cooled, chilled, then the layer of fat lifted off.

• If it has set, warm it to liquid form, then pour very slowly through a fine sieve, or a colander lined with cheesecloth. Transfer to a saucepan.

• Put the beef, chicken or fish on a board and hand-chop it finely, or chop in a food processor. Do not mince, because this crushes the fibres. Put the egg whites in a bowl and beat lightly, then stir in the beef, chicken or fish and the crushed shells. Stir well into the strained stock.

• Bring just to boiling point and simmer for 30 minutes without disturbing it – there should be a small blow-hole for the steam to escape. If there isn't one, make one with a spoon. Floating impurities will rise to the surface and stick to the albumen in the egg white mixture, forming an almost solid layer on top.

• Turn off the heat and carefully remove and discard this layer. Pour the clear liquid underneath through a strainer lined with cheesecloth and discard the solids.

beef consommé

1½ litres good Beef Stock (page 12), as clear as possible and with all fat removed

1 tablespoon port or sherry

1 tablespoon Madeira wine

salt, to taste

a sprig of chervil or some snipped chives, to serve

clarification

1 carrot, finely chopped

1 celery stalk, finely chopped

½ white onion, finely chopped

1 small leek, white part only, well cleaned and finely sliced

3 egg whites

crushed shells of 2 eggs

125 g beef, well trimmed of fat, then very finely hand-chopped or chopped in a food processor

serves 4

Consommés can be made with any stock – including chicken, duck, game or veal – though the most representative seems to me to be beef. Start with a carefully made stock, add an extra injection of flavour with chopped fresh vegetables and beef, then clarify in the traditional way, with chopped beef, egg whites and shells. The clarified stock is then served with various garnishes.

To prepare the clarification mixture, put the carrot, celery, onion, leek, egg whites, shells and chopped beef in a bowl and beat well. Transfer to a large saucepan, then add the stock and slowly bring to the boil over low heat. Stir constantly as it does so, to distribute the egg white thoroughly through the stock. As soon as it comes to the boil (about 10 minutes), immediately reduce to a simmer and stop stirring. The egg whites will rise very slowly to the surface, taking all the impurities with them.

After 15 minutes, turn off the heat and carefully spoon off the egg white layer from the surface. Line a large strainer with damp muslin and put over a bowl. Carefully ladle out the stock, avoiding the solids, letting it drip through the muslin into the bowl. Remove the strainer and taste the stock. Add a pinch of salt if necessary, then the sherry and Madeira.

Serve in consommé bowls with the simplest of garnishes – just a sprig of chervil or some snipped chives. To eat, the heat of the soup is tested with the spoon, then the consommé is drunk from the bowl, which has small handles.

Variations These are endless – use other kinds of stock, flavour with other ingredients, then top with shredded or sliced pieces of the main ingredient. Think of mushrooms, truffles, finely shredded vegetables, a little shredded chicken (as in the South-east Asian Chicken Soup with Vegetables on page 97) or cooked barley, tiny pasta or rice. Another variation is to add a small, lightly poached egg – perhaps bantam or quail (see page 122 for poaching method).

jellied consommés

Cubes of jellied consommés can be a delicious introduction to a summer lunch or cocktail party. I have included two here – one Western, one Eastern. The Western version is a flavourful stock set with gelatine, the Eastern one is set with agar-agar. In South-east Asia, agar-agar is used because it allows a mixture to set at temperatures over 3°C (37°F), so you don't need a refrigerator.

jellied consommé

Gelatine is available in 12 g sachets, powder or leaf form. One sachet, 1 tablespoon or 6 leaves of gelatine will set 3 cups of stock.

Put 60 ml cold water in a saucepan. Sprinkle the sachet or powdered gelatine over the top and let stand for 5 minutes to soften. Warm the stock over low heat, stir in the gelatine, and keep stirring until it has dissolved. Do not let boil. Remove from the heat and pour into a shallow metal baking tin. Let set, chill for 3 hours in the refrigerator. To serve, cut into squares and pile into soup bowls of serve in spoons as shown.

1 sachet or 1 tablespoon powdered gelatine or 6 leaves

750 ml well-flavoured beef consommé

1–2 shallow metal baking tins, lightly greased with vegetable oil

makes 1–2 tins

tomato chilli jellies with coriander

This is a great fingerfood for parties – serve in Chinese spoons. Though this recipe could be set with gelatine, try it with agar-agar. To set 750 ml liquid, you'll need 1 tablespoon powder or 3 tablespoons flakes. It comes in other forms, but these are the easiest to use. I like freshly squeezed tomato juice (for which you'll need a juicer), because commercial tomato juice is too thick.

Put the tomatoes through the juicer (only powerful juicers can deal with tomatoes). Pour into a saucepan, then add the salt and chillies. Bring the juice to the boil, then simmer for about 3 minutes. The froth will rise to the surface.

Remove from the heat, strain into a bowl and let cool. Reserve the chillies but discard the froth. When cool, add the agar-agar, stir well, then bring to the boil, stirring, until the agar-agar dissolves.

Transfer to a jug. Pour a little tomato juice into each container of the ice cube trays, add a slice of chilli, then more juice. Add a leaf of coriander, then top up with more tomato juice. Let set (you can put it in the refrigerator, though it doesn't need it).

To serve, dip the ice cube trays in warm water, then pop out the cubes and serve on Chinese spoons.

1½ kg ripe tomatoes, producing 750 ml juice

a large pinch of salt

2 small red chillies, deseeded and finely sliced

1 tablespoon agar-agar powder or 3 tablespoons flakes

a small bunch of coriander

an electric juicer

ice cube trays

makes about 2 trays

indian rasam
lemon pepper water

50 g toor dhaal (yellow lentils)

1 green chilli, slit and deseeded

a pinch of ground turmeric

350 g tomatoes (sour not sweet, if possible) chopped

1 tablespoon peanut oil

1 teaspoon mustard seeds

1 red chilli, split and deseeded

10 curry leaves (optional)

a pinch of asafoetida

4 garlic cloves, crushed

2 teaspoons black peppercorns

150 ml freshly squeezed lemon juice, from about 3 large lemons

salt

to serve

coriander leaves

3 cm fresh ginger, peeled and finely sliced into fine matchsticks

grated zest of 1 unwaxed lemon

serves 4

Asafoetida, a favourite Indian spice, is sold in Asian shops and specialist spice shops (page 126)

It's odd that India doesn't really go in for soup. But what about mulligatawny, do I hear you ask? Mulligatawny isn't Indian – it's Raj. And I have to say, its name is enough to put anyone off.

Rasam, on the other hand, is somewhere between a drink and a penance by fire, and is as close as they get to a soup on the subcontinent. It's served in the iron tumbler called a *lota*. I was given this recipe by Chef Praveen Anand, a man passionate about collecting and preserving the regional recipes of India. He showed me how to make this in the Sheraton in Madras, a city which has given up its Raj name and is now known by its proper Tamil name, Chennai.

Put the dhaal in a saucepan, add the chilli, turmeric, salt and 750 ml water. Bring to the boil and simmer until the lentils are soft. Remove the chilli and transfer the rest to a blender. Blend until smooth. Add the tomatoes to the blender and grind to a purée.

Crush the peppercorns with a mortar and pestle.

Heat the oil in a small pan, add the mustard seeds, red chilli and curry leaves, if using, and stir-fry for about 10 seconds. Stir in the asafoetida, garlic and salt. Add the blended tomato mixture, pepper, lemon juice and 750 ml water. Bring to the boil, then strain into a bowl and let cool. Discard the residue.

Taste and adjust the seasoning, let cool, chill and serve topped with coriander, ginger and lemon zest.

Note The rasam may be served hot or cold, but I loved the contrast of fiery hot rasam and the cold, misted metal of the *lota*.

clear japanese soup
with prawns, citrus and pepper

There are three main kinds of Japanese soups; the miso soups with tofu and wakame served as a 'drink' with sushi or sashimi; the big soups, such as New Year Soup; and these – clear dashi in which floats one to three beautiful ingredients, each a complement to the other.

4 shelled medium uncooked prawns, with tail fins intact

4 thin strips of citrus peel, such as yuzu if available, tied in a knot, or a slice of carrot or other vegetable, blanched

1 litre First Dashi (page 17), hot but not boiling, or 1 litre hot water with dashi powder

4 leaves of Japanese herb, such as shiso, or a slice of spring onion

furikake seasoning, Japanese seven-spice, or black pepper, to serve

serves 4

Cut each prawn along the belly without cutting all the way through. Open it out flat. Make a small slit where the backbone would be if it were a fish. Thread the tail up and through the slit in the back, then fan out the tail fins.

Cut the citrus zest with a cannelle cutter. Put the zest and prawns in a bowl and pour over boiling water.

Put the hot dashi in 4 Japanese soup bowls, add 1 prawn, 1 knot of zest or a slice of vegetable and a herb. Put on the lid, then serve with a small dish of furikake seasoning, Japanese seven-spice or black pepper.

Variation Moon Floating through Mist

Such a beautiful name! Put 1½ litres dashi in a saucepan, add 2 tablespoons tamari (wheat-free) soy sauce and 2 tablespoons mirin (sweet rice wine for cooking). Heat to just below boiling point and set aside. Bring a large, shallow pan of water to the boil and reduce to simmering.

Put 4 small unshelled eggs in a bowl and cover with hot water from the tap. Leave for 1 minute. Pour off the water, then crack the eggs into a cup. Slide them carefully into the simmering water. Remove from the heat, cover with a lid and set aside for 4 minutes. Have a bowl of cold water ready, then remove the poached eggs with a slotted spoon and slip into the cold water to stop them cooking further. Reheat the pan of water.

For each person, use 1–3 fresh shiitake mushrooms, depending on size. Remove the tough stems and cut a cross in the tops. Add them to the boiling water and cook for about 4 minutes, then remove and drain. Divide the hot stock between 4 serving bowls, add a few sprigs of washed watercress, 1–3 mushrooms and a poached egg, then serve as in the main recipe.

cream soups

cream soups

Cream soups became hugely popular with home cooks after the introduction of the blender and food processor. Previously, devices such as the mouli or food mill (opposite) and the tamis or drum sieve (page 22) did the same job, but required a good deal more elbow grease. If you've ever tried to pass cooked berries through a sieve, you'll get the idea. The result is wonderful, but too much like hard work. The new kitchen appliances enjoyed almost instant success. I remember when I first got a food processor – my long-suffering flatmate lasted about a week before asking plaintively, 'Please could we have something that's not puréed?'

General framework for cooking traditional cream soups

• Heat the butter in a frying pan, add the chopped onion and fry gently until softened and transparent. Do not let it brown. Add the garlic if using and stir-fry until aromatic, but do not let it brown. Add the chosen vegetable and stir-fry it for a couple of minutes. In the case of green vegetables, this intensifies the colour. Alternatively, brush with oil and roast in the oven (page 36).

• Add a thickening agent. This can be diced potato, cooked chickpeas or dried beans, but can also be a flour-based béchamel or brown roux, such as on page 38.

• Add the stock, bring to the boil, season to taste and simmer gently until the vegetables are cooked.

• Transfer to a blender, food processor or mouli and blend to a purée. You may have to work in batches, according to the size of the container. If using a stick blender, do it directly in the saucepan, but take care you don't splash yourself with hot soup.

• If using a mouli, work in batches and grind over a bowl. This is one of the most effective instruments if you haven't skinned and deseeded tomatoes before cooking.

• Return to the saucepan and reheat before serving in a tureen or soup plates.

• Add whatever garnishes you have chosen and serve.

Note This chapter provides a range of variations on this general framework.

about 50 g butter or oil

1–2 onions, chopped

garlic, crushed (optional)

about 750 g of the main ingredient, such as broccoli (page 42) or mushrooms (page 38)

a thickening agent, such as potatoes (the number depends on how thin the main ingredient is), cooked or canned beans or chickpeas, or a roux made of flour and fat, usually butter, fried to a paste

liquid, such as stock or water, at least 250 ml per person

seasonings and flavourings such as spices or herbs

garnishes, such as croutons, herbs, a spoonful of unpuréed vegetable, or cream

a puréeing machine, such as a blender, food processor, hand-held stick blender, mouli or tamis (drum sieve)

serves 4

pumpkin and coconut soup

1 kg pumpkin, cut into wedges but unpeeled

2 large potatoes, cut into chunks

250 ml canned thick coconut milk

1 litre Chicken Stock (page 14)

sea salt and freshly ground black pepper

peanut oil, for roasting and greasing

to serve

4 red bird's eye chillies, finely sliced

fresh coconut, shaved with a vegetable peeler, about 2–4 tablespoons

freshly grated nutmeg (optional)

a baking sheet

serves 4

Pumpkin soup is a favourite in France, America and especially the Antipodes, where pumpkin is such a popular vegetable that is one of the three served with the Sunday roast. The soup version can be made with boiled or roasted pumpkin, with or without potatoes added. Adding coconut milk reflects Australia's new Asian face in food and culture. The result is sweet and creamy, and all it needs is a prickle of chilli to point up the flavour. Use butternut squash if you must – but we purists insist on the dense-fleshed real pumpkin with grey or green skin.

Brush the baking sheet with oil, add the pumpkin chunks and brush them with oil too. Cook in a preheated oven at 200°C (400°F) Gas 6 until browned outside and soft and fluffy inside, about 30 minutes, according to the size of the chunks. Scrape the flesh out of the skins and discard the skins. Alternatively, boil peeled pumpkin in lightly salted water until tender. Drain.

Boil or steam the potatoes until tender, then drain.

Put the pumpkin and potatoes in a blender, add seasoning, coconut milk and a ladle of hot stock. Purée until smooth and creamy, adding more stock if necessary. (You may have to work in batches, according to the size of your blender.)

Transfer to a clean saucepan, season to taste and reheat to just below boiling point. Ladle into heated soup bowls, top with the chillies, coconut shavings and a little nutmeg, if using, then serve.

cream of mushroom soup

A few dried porcini will give a stronger flavour to a soup made with regular cultivated mushrooms. Use large portobellos to give a deeper colour as well as flavour.

Put the dried porcini in a bowl, add 250 ml boiling water and let soak for at least 15 minutes. Heat the oil in a frying pan, add the fresh mushrooms and sauté until coloured but still firm. Reserve a few slices for serving.

Add the onion to the frying pan and sauté until softened, then add the garlic, nutmeg and parsley. Rinse any grit out of the porcini and strain their soaking liquid several times through muslin or a tea strainer. Add the liquid and the porcini to the pan. Bring to the boil, then transfer to a food processor. Add 2 ladles of the boiling stock, then pulse until creamy but still chunky.

Heat the butter in a saucepan, stir in the flour and cook gently, stirring constantly, until the mixture is very dark brown (take care or it will burn). Add the remaining stock, 1 ladle at a time, stirring well after each addition. Add the mushroom mixture, bring to the boil, then simmer for 20 minutes. Add salt and pepper to taste, then serve topped with a few reserved mushrooms, parsley, if using, and a spoonful of crème fraîche.

Notes If you use a blender to make soup, the purée will be very smooth. If you use a food processor, it will be less smooth, and if you use the pulse button, you can make the mixture quite chunky, which I think suits mushrooms.

*The browned flour and butter mixture (brown roux) gives a wonderful nutty aroma to the soup, and is used in some French and Italian recipes. You may omit it, but the flavour and texture it gives is wonderful.

25 g dried porcini mushrooms

4 tablespoons olive oil

6 large portobello mushrooms, wiped, trimmed and sliced

1 onion, halved and finely sliced

3 garlic cloves, crushed

a pinch of freshly grated nutmeg

leaves from a large bunch of parsley, finely chopped in a food processor

1¼ litres boiling Chicken (page 14) or Vegetable Stock (page 15)

4 tablespoons butter*

4 tablespoons plain flour*

sea salt and freshly ground black pepper

to serve

4–6 tablespoons coarsely chopped fresh parsley

4–6 tablespoons crème fraîche

serves 4–6

carrot vichyssoise

I like this soup cold, as well as hot. In fact its name is something of a pun. Vichyssoise is a cold soup of potatoes and leeks. In France, *carottes Vichy* is a famous carrot dish, so here we have them together. (In addition, Vichy water is a well-known brand of bottled water.) I like the pale pepperiness of ginger, because I'm not fond of white pepper. However, if you don't have any ginger on hand, substitute white pepper, but add it at the end, so it keeps its zing.

a large pinch of saffron threads

1 large leek, root end and green part trimmed and discarded

3 large carrots, about 500 g

2 large potatoes, about 350 g, cut into even pieces

500 ml Chicken Stock (page 14) or mineral water

2 tablespoons butter

2 tablespoons sunflower oil

2 garlic cloves, crushed

3 cm fresh ginger, peeled and finely grated

sea salt

to serve

4 tablespoons cream or crème fraîche

a handful of chives, scissor-snipped

serves 4

Put the saffron in a small cup and cover with about 125 ml boiling water. Let steep while you prepare the rest of the soup, but at least 20 minutes.

Split the leek in half and wash it well. Drain, pat dry with kitchen paper, then slice thinly into half-moons.

Grate the carrots on the large side of a box grater or in a food processor.

Put the potatoes in a saucepan, add the stock or water to cover and bring to the boil. Add a pinch of salt and simmer gently until done. Reserve the cooking liquid.

Meanwhile, melt the butter and olive oil in a frying pan, add the leeks and cook until softened but not browned in any way – they will become a green-gold colour. Transfer to a dish. Add a little more butter and oil to the pan, then the garlic, ginger and carrots. Simmer until done, then add the saffron and its soaking water. Transfer the leeks to the pan and simmer for about 5 minutes. Add the cooked potatoes and blend with a hand-held stick blender. Alternatively, you can mash them before adding to the soup, then blend. Stir in the potato cooking water. Taste, and add salt as necessary. Let simmer for a further 5 minutes to meld the colours and flavours.

The thickness of the soup will depend on the flouriness of the potatoes. Add liquid to thin to the desired consistency, but remember to adjust the seasonings.

Ladle into bowls, add a swirl of cream or a spoonful of crème fraîche, then snip fresh chives over the top.

To serve as a vichyssoise – a cold soup – let it cool after blending, then chill. The potatoes will thicken when cold, so you may need to add some more cold mineral water to thin it to the required consistency.

Variation If you prefer not to use potatoes, substitute 2 cans chickpeas, rinsed and drained. Press them through a mouli to remove the skins (which makes them more digestible). Alternatively, purée them with a ladle or two of the stock.

cream of broccoli soup
with leeks and broad beans

2 large leeks

2 tablespoons butter

2 tablespoons sunflower oil

2 large heads broccoli, broken into florets

1 medium baking potato, chopped

600 ml Vegetable (page 15) or Chicken Stock (page 14)

250 g shelled broad beans, fresh or frozen

sea salt and freshly ground white pepper

basil or parsley oil (page 123), to serve

serves 4

A pale green, fresh, summery soup that can be adapted to other ingredients – it's also good with cauliflower and cannellini beans, or sweet potatoes and fresh borlottis. Feel free to use frozen broad beans. Like peas and corn, they are one of the few ingredients that can be better frozen. Picked and frozen almost immediately, their sugars have no time to turn to starch.

Cut off and discard the roots and most of the green from the leeks. Split them lengthways and wash carefully (grit works its way down between the leaves). Chop coarsely, then put in a salad spinner and spin dry.

Put the butter and oil in a large saucepan and heat until the butter melts. Add the leeks and fry gently until softened but not browned. Reserve a few spoonfuls of the cooked leeks for garnish.

Add the broccoli to the pan and stir-fry until bright green. Add the potato and stock and bring to the boil. Reduce the heat, add salt and pepper and simmer for 30 minutes, topping up with boiling water if necessary.

If using broad beans, cook in boiling salted water until just tender, then drain and transfer to a bowl of cold water. Pop the cooked beans out of their grey skins and discard the skins – the bright green beans look and taste better. Reserve a few spoonfuls of broad beans for serving.

Strain the soup into a bowl and put the solids and remaining broad beans in a blender or food processor. Add 2 ladles of the strained liquid and purée until smooth. Add the remaining liquid and blend again. If the soup is too thick, thin it with water. Reheat the soup, pour into heated soup bowls, top with the reserved leeks and skinned broad beans, then serve with a trickle of basil or parsley oil over the top.

Note If you like, the potato may be omitted. Instead, peel the broccoli stalks, chop coarsely and add at the same time as the stock.

bisque

1 packet Chinese dried shrimp,
about 50 g

a large pinch of saffron threads or
1 sachet powdered saffron (optional)

2 tablespoons olive oil

2 large shallots, chopped

2 garlic cloves, crushed

at least 500 g cooked lobster or crab
shells, well broken, or prawn shells

1 litre Fish Stock (page 14)

1 fresh bay leaf

2 tablespoons harissa paste

500 g boneless white fish fillets,
such as cod

freshly squeezed juice of ½ lemon

sea salt and freshly ground
black pepper

to serve (optional)

toast and rouille (pages 101 and 120)

125 g freshly grated cheese,
such as Gruyère

serves 4

A bisque is a soup made with the shells of seafood such as prawns, crabs or lobster – and a blender or food processor is the easiest way to make it. Whenever you have lobster or crab, keep the shells and bits, and break them into smaller pieces with a meat mallet or rolling pin, or a large Thai-style mortar and pestle. Keep them in the freezer until you have enough, because I can't deny that these shellfish are very expensive creatures. However, sometimes I just can't wait, and find that Chinese dried shrimp give tons of extra flavour for very little money.

Put the dried shrimp and saffron threads, if using, in a small bowl and cover with boiling water. Set aside until the shrimp soften, about 20 minutes.

Heat the oil in a large, heavy-based saucepan, add the shallots and sauté until softened and translucent. Add the garlic and seafood shells and stir-fry until aromatic. Add the stock, bay leaf, dried shrimp and saffron and their soaking liquid. Boil hard for about 5 minutes so the stock and oil amalgamate. Add the harissa and fish and poach for 5 minutes until the fish is opaque.

Remove the bay leaf, strain the soup into a bowl or jug and transfer the solids, including the shells, to a food processor. This is hard labour for the blades, so work in batches and use the metal ones. Add 1–2 ladles of stock and blend until smooth. Push the mixture through a strainer into the rinsed saucepan, then transfer the solids back into the blender. Add more stock, blend again and push through a strainer again. Repeat until all the stock has been used. The more you blend and push, the stronger the flavour will be.

Discard the solids in the strainer and reheat the soup in the saucepan. Stir in the lemon juice and salt to taste. Add pepper if you like, then serve. Toast and rouille and some grated cheese would also be delicious with this soup.

vegetables

french onion soup

This was the porters' favourite dish in the great Paris market of Les Halles. I was there years ago, after the market had moved, and there were still places selling bowls of this fortifying brew to visitors. Then – and ever since – I burned my mouth by being much too greedy to wait for it to cool down to eating temperature. Beware!

50 g unsalted butter, preferably clarified, plus extra butter to finish

1 tablespoon olive oil

1 kg onions, thinly sliced

1 teaspoon salt

50 g plain flour

1 litre Beef Stock (page 12), or Beef and Chicken mixed (pages 12 and 14)

sea salt and freshly ground black pepper

to finish

8–12 thick slices of bread (about 2 cm)

1 tablespoon olive oil

1 large garlic clove, halved

125 g. Gruyère cheese, freshly grated

serves 4–6

Put the butter and oil in a large saucepan or stockpot and heat until the butter melts. Add the onions and salt and stir well. Cook over low heat for 20–30 minutes or until the onions are golden brown. Do not increase the heat, or the butter will burn. Sprinkle the flour over the onions and stir for 2–3 minutes until there is no sign of white specks of flour (if you leave them, they will appear as lumps in the final soup).

Heat the stock in a separate saucepan, then pour 1–2 ladles onto the onions. Stir well, then add the remaining stock and simmer, part-covered, for another 20–30 minutes. Add salt and pepper to taste.

Meanwhile, put the bread on a baking sheet and toast in a preheated oven at 160°C (325°F) Gas 3 for about 15 minutes. Brush with the olive oil and rub with the cut garlic clove, return to the oven for another 15 minutes or until the bread is quite dry (if you put undried bread in the soup it will turn to mush).

To serve, ladle the soup into 6 onion soup bowls.*

Put the slices of toast (the croutes) on top and pile the cheese over them. Dot with more butter and cook at the same temperature for about 15 minutes until the cheese is melted. Put under a preheated grill to brown the top for 1–2 minutes if you like.

*Note The little bowls shown here, with pedestal foot and lion's head handles, are the traditional onion soup dishes, made by Pillivuyt and Apilco, two of the great French porcelain makers. Use a pudding spoon to eat from them – a soup spoon is too big.

tomato soup

1 kg very ripe red tomatoes

500 ml Chicken Stock (page 14), or to taste

sea salt and coarsely crushed black pepper

to serve (optional)

shredded zest and freshly squeezed juice of 1 unwaxed lemon

4 tablespoons pesto

scissor-snipped chives or torn basil

serves 4

My sister is a farmer in Australia and, among other things, grows great tomatoes. So good, in fact, that her farm has won awards from magazines and accolades from food writers for the flavour and quality of her produce. I used to go there for the summer holidays, and we would spend at least one day pressing and preserving tomatoes for me to take back to the city. A couple of her big, strong sons turned the grinder as we packed two-litre preserving jars with the results of their labours. For the rest of the year, to impress guests, all I had to do was decant a jar or two into a saucepan, thin down with stock, heat until almost but not quite boiling (otherwise it loses its fresh taste), then add lemon juice and zest or a spoonful of pesto.

To skin the tomatoes, cut a cross in the base of each and dunk into a saucepan of boiling water. Remove after 10 seconds and put into a strainer set over a large saucepan. Slip off and discard the skins and cut the tomatoes in half around their 'equators'. Using a teaspoon, deseed into the strainer, then press the pulp and juice through the strainer and add to the blender. Discard the seeds. Chop the tomato halves and add to the blender. Alternatively, put through a tomato grinder or a mouli food mill (page 34).

Purée the tomatoes, adding a little of the stock to help the process – you may have to work in batches. Add the remaining stock, season to taste and transfer to the saucepan. Heat well without boiling. Serve in heated soup plates topped with a spoonful of lemon juice, pesto if using, chives or basil, lemon zest and pepper.

soupe au pistou

Pistou is the Provençal version of pesto, and to make it you need a big bunch of scented summertime basil. Unlike pesto, it doesn't contain pine nuts or cheese. This version of the soup is quicker to cook than the traditional one, because I prefer the vegetables to have the flavour and texture best suited to that variety. If you'd like the classic, cook it all together – beans first (page 75); then root vegetables and pasta; then fresh peas, followed by leafy things. Red kidney beans are often included, but I like white beans better.

To make the pistou, put the basil and garlic in a blender or food processor and blend as finely as possible. Add enough olive oil in a steady stream to form a loose paste. Set aside.

Heat the oil in a small frying pan, add the onion wedges and fry gently on both sides until softened. Cook the potato and soup pasta in boiling salted water until tender. Drain. Blanch your choice of carrots, sprouts, courgettes, pepper and peas, in boiling salted water until tender but crisp, about 3–5 minutes. Drain and refresh in cold water.

Bring the stock to the boil and add the seasoning, pasta and all vegetables including the cannellini beans. Simmer for 2 minutes or until heated through.

Serve in heated soup plates, with a separate bowl of pistou. Guests stir the pistou into their soup to taste.

4 tablespoons olive oil

1 red onion, cut into wedges

1 large potato, cut into 1 cm cubes

a handful (about 125 g) of soup pasta, such as orecchetti (or the traditional vermicelli)

1 litre Chicken (page 14) or Vegetable Stock (page 15)

250 g cooked or canned cannellini beans, rinsed and drained

4 baby carrots, halved or quartered lengthways

250 g Brussels sprouts, halved, or baby courgettes, cut into thick slices

1 red pepper, peeled, cored and sliced

250 g shelled green peas

sea salt and freshly ground black pepper

pistou

leaves from 1 large bunch of basil

2 garlic cloves, crushed

olive oil (see method)

serves 4

iced beetroot soup
with crème fraîche and vodka

This soup is a surprise – the layer of crème fraîche underneath the beetroot soup is invisible until you put your spoon in (and it also helps hold up the cucumber). The recipe was given to me by Frederick, who is French and a wine merchant. Unlike many of his compatriots, he loves New World wines, but seems to have had a brainstorm this day and opted for vodka. This is my version of Frederick's soup, and it's delicious.

500 g cooked beetroot, chopped

750 ml Chicken (page 14) or Beef Stock (page 12)

1 tablespoon harissa paste, or to taste

sea salt and freshly ground black pepper

to serve

1 mini (Lebanese) cucumber or about 10 cm regular cucumber

250 ml crème fraîche

ice cubes (optional)

freshly grated lemon zest or 4 teaspoons caviar (optional)

iced vodka

serves 4

Put the beetroot in a blender, add 2 ladles of stock and purée until smooth. Add the remaining stock and purée again. Test for thickness, then add the harissa paste and salt and pepper to taste, adding extra stock or water if the purée is too thick. Blend again, then chill very well. Chill all the remaining ingredients.

To prepare the cucumber, cut off the ends and slice thinly on a mandoline or with a vegetable peeler. Cut it diagonally, or into rounds, or in cubes, as you like. If using a regular cucumber, cut the slices in quarters.

When ready to serve, put a layer of crème fraîche in each chilled serving bowl and spread it flat with the back of a spoon. Carefully pour the beetroot soup over the back of another spoon so it doesn't disturb the cream. Add a few ice cubes to each serving if you like (Frederick doesn't). Put a few pieces of cucumber in the middle – the cream will hold them up – then sprinkle with a very little finely grated lemon zest, if using. Serve with a shot of iced vodka.

Variation Jellied Beetroot Soup

Beetroot soups are also wonderful jellied. Following the relative quantities given for Jellied Consommé on page 27, soak the gelatine in cold water until softened. Strain the beetroot soup into a saucepan, warm gently and add the gelatine. Heat gently, without boiling, until the gelatine has dissolved. Strain through muslin again and let cool. Pour into a rectangular plastic dish, cover and chill until set.

To serve, heat a tablespoon, scoop out egg-shaped spoonfuls and put them in bowls. Top with a spoonful of sour cream, a teaspoon of caviar and chopped chives.

minestrone

200 g dried cannellini beans

250 g smoked pancetta or bacon, cut into cubes or strips

2 garlic cloves, crushed

2 large stalks of parsley, lightly crushed

1 tablespoon olive oil

1 large onion, chopped

2 large potatoes, cubed and rinsed

3 carrots, cubed

2 celery stalks, sliced

3 tomatoes, halved, deseeded and chopped

200 g Italian risotto rice

1 small round cabbage, quartered, cored and sliced

250 g shelled peas, fresh or frozen

3 small courgettes, halved lengthways, halved again into quarters, then thickly sliced

sea salt and freshly ground black pepper

to serve

a handful of basil, torn

crusty Italian bread

a dish of freshly grated Parmesan cheese

serves 6–8

There are as many versions of minestrone (big soup) as there are regions of Italy – and Italian grandmothers. I am told that tomatoes, garlic, oil and pasta are used in southern recipes, beans in soups from central Italy, and rice in the north. In Genoa they add a spoonful of pesto, in Tuscany the soup is poured over their chunky unsalted bread, and in other areas, pork or bacon in various forms is added. I love smoked pancetta and bacon, so I have used both, plus olive oil because it gives flavour to an already flavourful soup (and vegetables love it).

Soak the beans overnight in at least 1¼ litres cold water to cover (pages 74–5).

Drain, then put in a saucepan, cover with cold water and bring to the boil. Reduce the heat and simmer until almost tender (they will be cooked again, so don't let them get too soft). Do not add salt during this precooking, or you will have cannellini bullets. Drain and set aside.

Put the pancetta, garlic and parsley in a stockpot, heat gently and fry until the fat runs. Add the olive oil, heat briefly, then add the onion and cook gently until softened but not browned.

Add the potatoes, carrots, celery, tomatoes, salt and pepper. Add 3 litres water and heat until simmering. Cook over low heat for about 20 minutes. Add the rice and simmer for 10 minutes. Add the cabbage and reserved beans, bring to the boil and cook for 5 minutes, then add the peas and courgettes and cook for another 2–3 minutes until all the vegetables are tender. Remove and discard the parsley stalks, add salt and pepper to taste, then serve sprinkled with torn basil. Crusty Italian bread and freshly grated Parmesan is, of course, the perfect accompaniment.

Note If you would like to use canned beans, do so, but remember that they often have sugar and salt added, so keep that in mind when seasoning. They are already quite soft, so add them at the end and cook only until heated through. I like the ones sold in large bottles rather than cans.

gazpacho

The classic summer soup of Spain has dozens of variations, depending on its area of origin. The traditional way of serving is in a tureen with 6 separate dishes of garnishes – these are added by the guests, according to taste. Chop each ingredient coarsely, rather than finely – the soup should have some texture. I have departed from the original recipe because I prefer small Lebanese cucumbers, which have fewer seeds, more flesh and nicer skin. I also prefer harissa paste rather than tomato paste and to omit the bread in the blended section – but my Spanish friend tells me this is sacrilege.

4 Lebanese cucumbers, halved lengthways, deseeded, peeled and chopped*

6 tomatoes, skinned and chopped

1 large red onion, chopped

1 red pepper, deseeded and chopped

1 garlic clove, finely chopped

125 g bread, crusts removed (optional)

3 tablespoons red wine vinegar

3 teaspoons salt

3 tablespoons olive oil

1 tablespoon tomato purée or harissa paste

to serve

3 thick slices good bread, crusts removed, cut into cubes

1 onion, finely chopped

1–2 Lebanese cucumbers, halved, deseeded and chopped (skin left on)

1 green or red pepper, deseeded and finely chopped

2 hard-boiled eggs, chopped

2 ripe tomatoes, halved, deseeded and chopped

olive oil, for frying

serves 6

Put the peeled cucumbers, tomatoes, onion, pepper, garlic, bread, if using, vinegar and salt into a food processor (which gives more texture than a blender). Add 1 litre iced water and blend until coarsely chopped, in batches if necessary, then ladle into a bowl. Mix the olive oil and harissa paste in a small bowl, then whisk it into the soup. Chill until ready to serve, but at least 3 hours.

Meanwhile, heat some olive oil in a frying pan, add the bread cubes and sauté, turning frequently, until crisp and golden on all sides. Watch them, because they burn easily. Remove from the pan, drain on kitchen paper and reserve.

When ready to serve, put each garnish in a separate small bowl, with a spoon.

Serve the soup in the tureen or in soup plates, for guests to add their own garnishes.

*Note I peel the cucumbers and use a red pepper, not green, in the soup, because I think red and green blended together makes a rather unappetizing greyish-brown. However, to be authentic, use these green elements.

peas, beans and lentils

swedish yellow pea soup

This is my own version of a hearty Scandinavian soup. Often, it has no meat in it – and uses celeriac instead. So if one of those ugly, hard-to-get-on-with roots appears in your market, halve it, peel it (carefully) and cut into cubes, adding at the same time as the peas. I prefer this soup made with smoked pork knuckle, available from real butchers. For some reason, old Scandinavian cookbooks tell you to soak the peas overnight. You can if you like, but since they're split, they have no coating to be softened. never do. If you can't find yellow split peas in your supermarket, try an Indian one and buy yellow channa dhaal, but not the oiled ones.

1 smoked pork knuckle or ham hock

500 g yellow split peas

2 onions, halved lengthways

6 cloves, stuck in the onions

1 carrot, thickly sliced

3 fresh bay leaves

3 long curls of orange zest

4 tablespoons Dijon mustard

salt (optional – see method) and freshly ground black pepper

snipped chives or parsley, to serve

serves 4

Put the pork knuckle in a snug-fitting saucepan and cover it with cold water. Bring to the boil, reduce the heat and simmer until tender. Skim it from time to time and top up with more boiling water as necessary. When done, the meat will fall easily off the bone. Drain, remove the skin and bone and pull the meat into bite-sized shreds, small enough to fit easily on a soup spoon. Reserve 250 ml of the cooking liquid.

Rinse the peas in cold running water and put in a large saucepan. Add the onions stuck with cloves, the carrot, bay leaves, orange zest and 1 litre water. Bring to the boil, reduce the heat and simmer until done, about 30 minutes.

The peas should be soft, but still keep their shape. If not, cook for 5–10 minutes more – the time will depend on the age of the peas. Remove the cloves, bay leaves, orange zest and (optional) the onions and carrot. If you would like a smoother texture, the peas can be puréed in a blender or food processor, in batches if necessary.

Return the peas to the saucepan, stir in the mustard and pork shreds and taste for seasoning. Instead of salt, I like to add a little of the reserved liquid used to cook the pork. It will be salty and meaty – take care, it's easy to add too much. Serve sprinkled with scissor-snipped herbs.

minestra di farro

2–4 tablespoons olive oil

1 carrot, finely chopped

1 onion, chopped

1–2 garlic cloves, crushed

500 g farro mixture*

1 bay leaf

1 litre Chicken (page 14) or
Vegetable Stock (page 15)

sea salt and freshly ground black pepper

to serve

grated cheese

olive oil

serves 4

Soup mixes like this one are sold in every Italian supermarket, but I've found that in other parts of the world, they're never so interesting and exciting. If you prefer, make your own from whatever you have in your collection of dried peas, beans, lentils and grains. Spelt, the major grain in the mix, is a very ancient wheat, which is also used to make bread. It is said to be more acceptable to those who are wheat intolerant. Some people prefer barley or other grains. If you're in an Italian deli, try to buy the real farro mixture, usually sold in 500 g packets.

Heat the olive oil in a large saucepan, add the carrot and onion and cook slowly until softened but not browned. Add the garlic and cook until softened.

Add the farro mixture, bay leaf and stock and bring to the boil. Simmer slowly until done, about 30 minutes. Season with salt and pepper after 20 minutes.

Ladle into soup bowls, then serve with a a bowl of grated cheese and some best olive oil for people to add a swirl themselves.

***Note** To make your own mixture, use 200 g farro (spelt) or pearl barley, 100 g yellow split peas, 100 g green split peas and 100 g baby white beans (fagiolini). Soak the baby beans overnight in cold water before using.

flag bean soup

1 tablespoon olive oil, plus extra to taste

3 large garlic cloves,
2 cut into slices, 1 crushed

1 large onion, finely chopped

250 g Puy lentils

1 litre boiling Chicken (page 14) or
Vegetable Stock (page 15),
plus extra to taste

100 g canned butter beans

200 g canned green flageolet beans

200 g canned red kidney beans

200 g canned haricot or cannellini beans

sea salt and freshly ground black pepper

to serve

parsley or basil leaves

basil oil (page 123), or olive oil

grated lemon zest (optional)

crusty bread

serves 4

I've dubbed this 'flag soup' because the beans are red, green and white, the colour of the Italian flag. This is the sort of soup you need on a cold winter's day. Using canned beans, it takes no time at all to prepare, and you can use vegetable or chicken stock, according to whether your audience is vegetarian or not. My friend Luana, who must be the only vegetarian in all of Italy, gave me this idea – she brings it to work for lunch and serves it with crusty bread. If you would like to prepare the soup from dried beans, use the information on pages 74–5.

Heat the oil in a frying pan, add the sliced garlic and fry gently on both sides until crisp and golden. Remove and drain on kitchen paper.

Add the onion and crushed garlic to the frying pan, adding extra oil if necessary, and cook gently until softened and transparent. Add the lentils and half the boiling stock and cook until the lentils are just tender.

Meanwhile, rinse and drain all the beans. Put them in a sieve and dunk the sieve in a large saucepan of boiling water. The beans are cooked – you are just reheating them.

Add the hot beans to the lentils and add the remaining stock. Taste, and add salt and pepper as necessary. If the soup is too thick, add extra boiling stock or water. Ladle into bowls, top with the reserved fried garlic and the herbs, add a few drops of basil oil and the lemon zest, if using, then serve with crusty bread.

red lentil and chorizo soup

Red lentils have the advantage of cooking quickly into a beautifully coloured purée. They carry other flavours in a most delicious way. Top them with chorizo, the cooking kind, about 2 cm in diameter – the very spicy ones are strung with red cord, the sweet ones with white cord. I prefer white, because then you can add other flavours without adding too much pain.

Heat 3 tablespoons of the olive oil in a large saucepan, add the onion, carrot and celery and sauté until softened but not browned. Add the garlic and ginger and sauté until the garlic has softened but is not browned. Stir in the paprika, then add the lentils and stir to cover with the flavourings. Add the stock. Bring to the boil and simmer until the lentils are tender – they will turn into a purée.

Meanwhile, heat the remaining oil in a frying pan, add the chorizo slices in a single layer and fry until they are lightly browned, and turn inside out, like tiny bowls. They will be crisp and brown on the underside. Turn them over and lightly fry the other side until crisp. Remove to a plate until ready to serve. Keep the frying oil.

Test the texture of the lentil soup – if too thick, stir in extra boiling stock or water. Ladle into bowls, top with the chorizo and parsley, and spoon the reserved frying oil over the top – it will be a brilliant orange-red.

4 tablespoons olive oil

1 onion, finely chopped

1 large carrot, cubed

1 celery stalk, cubed

2 garlic cloves, crushed

3 cm fresh ginger, grated

½ teaspoon smoked sweet Spanish paprika

500 g red lentils

1 litre Chicken Stock (page 14)

2–3 chorizos (see recipe introduction), finely sliced

2 tablespoons coarsely chopped flat leaf parsley

serves 4

fresh pea soup
with mint and crispy bacon

One of the great classics of the soup world is Pea and Ham Soup. We made it at the end of the Christmas holidays, when only the bone and a few shreds of meat were left from the ham. These were cooked with dried green peas and water to form a lovely, comforting, warming winter soup. But, since Christmas in Australia is boiling hot, this was more a matter of tradition than sense, so this is a modern version using fresh or frozen peas (and you don't have to eat an entire ham first).

1 tablespoon olive oil

4–8 slices very thinly cut smoked pancetta or smoked streaky bacon

500 g shelled peas, fresh or frozen

1 litre boiling ham stock, Chicken Stock (page 14) or water

sea salt and freshly ground black pepper

to serve

4 tablespoons single cream

sprigs of mint

serves 4

Heat the olive oil in a frying pan, add the pancetta and sauté until crisp. Remove and drain on crumpled kitchen paper, or drape over a wooden spoon so they curl.

To cook the peas, microwave on HIGH for 3–4 minutes, or follow the package instructions. Alternatively, simmer in boiling water with a pinch of salt for 2–3 minutes or until tender. Drain.

Put the peas in a blender with 1–2 ladles of boiling stock or water. Work to a purée, adding extra stock if necessary. Add the remaining stock and blend again. Taste and adjust the seasoning. Reheat, thinning with a little boiling water if necessary, then ladle into heated soup bowls and serve, topped with the crisp bacon, a swirl of cream and sprigs of mint.

Variation Cook the peas, drain and let cool, then put in the blender with 8 ice cubes and enough water to make the blades run. Blend to a purée, then thin with iced water to the consistency you like. Add salt and pepper to taste and serve topped with sliced spring onions.

japanese miso soup

1 tub silken tofu

50 g dried wakame seaweed*

1 litre First Dashi (page 17)

3 tablespoons dark miso paste

1 tablespoon white miso paste

1 spring onion, chopped

serves 4

Japanese ingredients are now widely available, but if you can't find wakame, a few sprigs of watercress would taste delicious.

Miso pastes, widely used in Japanese soups, are made from soy beans, and so is the tofu in this soup. There are many flavours and varieties of miso, but there are three main versions, with cultures based on barley, rice and soy beans. All three are easy to find, either in the Japanese or sushi section of larger supermarkets, or in health food stores. The tofu used here is the elegant silken kind. Before cutting the block into pieces, let it drain between two small plates – the weight of the top one will force out some of the liquid and make it easier to cut (you can also put a small food can on the top plate to help it along).

Remove the tofu from its container and slide it out onto a small plate. Put another plate on top and set aside for 30 minutes to press out some of the liquid.

Put the wakame in a bowl of water and let soften. Cut out any stiff sections with scissors and discard. Cut the wakame into 3 cm strips.

Put the dashi in a saucepan, bring almost to the boil, then reduce to a simmer. Set a strainer over the saucepan and add the miso. Using the back of a ladle, press the miso into the dashi and reduce the heat so the soup doesn't boil.

Add the wakame and simmer for 2 minutes.

Cut the tofu in half through its thickness. Cut into 1 cm cubes and drop into the soup (it is easier to do this if you hold the tofu cake in your palm and slice it carefully – it is very fragile). When the tofu floats to the surface, like ravioli, it is cooked. Carefully ladle into soup bowls, sprinkle the spring onion over the top and serve.

Note This is the traditional accompaniment to sushi and similar dishes. The soup is drunk at the end – eat the tofu and wakame with chopsticks, then pick up the bowl and sip. (The rim and foot are specially designed not to be heat-conductors, so you won't burn yourself.)

preparing dried peas, beans and lentils

Canned pulses are quick, convenient and taste almost as good as the ones you soak and cook yourself. However, they often contain added sugar and salt and some people prefer to add their own. The texture is often different too, especially for white beans. Red kidney beans, on the other hand, seem to look beautifully coloured and glossy when they come out of a can, and buying them ready-cooked eliminates any worries about boiling for 10 minutes to remove the toxins.

soaking

- There is no need to soak lentils or split peas before cooking. However, whole peas do need soaking in the same way as beans.

- Soak dried beans before cooking to soften them and reduce the cooking time. The other great advantage of soaking is that it removes a large percentage of gas-producing enzymes.

- Soak them in 5 times their volume of water – hot or cold.

hot soaking

- Rinse and drain the beans. For each 250 g beans, add 1¼ litres water; bring to the boil for 2–3 minutes, then remove from the heat and let soak for 1–4 hours. Hot soaking is said to remove more gas-producing enzymes than cold.

- Rinse and drain the soaked beans, then cook as described below.

cold soaking

- For each 250 g beans, put them in a bowl, add 1¼ litres cold water; and let soak for at least 8 hours or overnight.

cooking

Drain the beans, rinse and drain again. Put in a saucepan, add 1¼ litres cold water and bring to the boil. Reduce the heat and simmer for the length of time listed below or until tender (the precise time will depend on the age of the beans and even where they were grown).

- Aromatics may be added, but DO NOT ADD salt, tomatoes, wine or lemon juice until the very end of cooking time, otherwise the beans will stay hard.

- Don't add bicarbonate of soda, as is traditional in some cuisines. It wrecks the taste and nutritional value.

- To test if the beans are cooked, bite and taste. A famous test is to remove a spoonful from the pot and blow on them. Their skins will split when they're done. Keep the beans in their cooking liquid until ready to use.

- Pressure cooking is popular with people who cook beans all the time. Consult the manufacturer's handbook for the best way of cooking beans in your appliance.

Note Canned beans are already soaked and cooked, so don't recook them. They can be used cold, or reheated in a dish. Rinse and drain thoroughly before use. (Check the use-by date before using.)

storing

Store dried beans in dry place, preferably in a sealed container, and use as soon as possible after buying. They keep well, whatever their age, but younger ones cook more quickly.

Cooked beans will keep in a covered container in the refrigerator for several days. They also freeze well. Rose Elliot in *The Bean Book* recommends doing this particularly for the varieties that take a long time to cook.

how many, how much?

250 g dried beans will produce
750 ml cooked beans

500 g dried beans will produce
1½ litres cooked beans

500 g dried beans is the same as
500 ml dried beans

500 g canned beans produces
350 ml cooked, drained beans

cooking times

Lentils (unsoaked)

French Puy lentils	about 30 minutes
Red lentils	about 30 minutes
Green or brown lentils	about 30 minutes
Whole black lentils (urid dhaal)	30 minutes, after soaking
Split white lentils (urid dhaal)	about 30 minutes
Yellow lentils (channa dhaal)	about 30 minutes

Peas

Split peas (green or yellow)	40 minutes (unsoaked)
Whole peas	30 minutes (soaked)

Beans

Adzuki beans	30 minutes
Black beans	1 hour
Black-eyed beans	30–45 minutes
Borlotti beans	1 hour
Broad beans	
Egyptian ful medames	1–4 hours
Regular dried broad beans	1½ hours
Spanish fave beans	Cook 4 hours after soaking at least 24 hours
Butter (lima) beans	1¼ hours if small, 1–1½ hours if large
Cannellini beans	1 hour
Chickpeas	1–1½ hours. *Note* If using to make felafels, soak only, do not boil.
Flageolet beans (green)	45–60 minutes
Haricot beans	45–60 minutes
Mung beans	30 minutes
Pinto beans	1–1¼ hours
Red kidney beans	Boil hard 10 minutes, then drain, rinse and drain again to remove toxins, then cook 1½–2 hours.
Soy beans	Contain a trypsin inhibitor (preventing assimilation of amino acid methionine). This is destroyed by soaking for at least 12 hours. Drain, rinse, then drain again. Boil hard for 1 hour, then simmer for 2–3 hours.

eggs

chinese egg drop soup

One of the great classics of Chinese soupery, at least in Western restaurants, this soup is thickened with a mixture of cornflour and water, that great standby of Chinese cooking. The variation, Chicken and Sweetcorn Soup, is equally familiar to restaurant-goers. Corn is now so much a part of Chinese cooking that you wonder what they did before it arrived from the New World. Use fresh corn scraped straight off the cob if available, otherwise, frozen corn is the next best option. White pepper is commonly used in Chinese cooking and I think black would ruin the appearance of this fresh soup.

1 teaspoon cornflour

1 litre Chinese Stock made with chicken (page 16)

2 large eggs, beaten

2 large spring onions, the white and some of the green, thinly sliced

sea salt and freshly ground white pepper

serves 4

Put the cornflour in a cup and stir in 3–4 tablespoons cold water. Stir until the mixture is smooth – any lumps will remain as lumps in the final soup.

Put the stock and a pinch of salt in a saucepan and bring to the boil. Taste, adding more salt if necessary. Stir in the cornflour and let thicken for about 1 minute. Don't cook too long or the cornflour will lose its thickening properties.

While whisking the soup, slowly pour in the beaten egg in a thin stream (use a jug for ease). The egg will form threads in the soup. Serve in hot bowls sprinkled with the spring onions and pepper.

Variation Chicken and Sweetcorn Soup

Mix the cornflour with water as in the main recipe, stirring again just before you add it.

Chop or shred 250 g cooked chicken breast into bite-sized pieces. Bring the chicken stock to the boil.

Remove and discard the husks and silks from 2 fresh ears of corn. Put them, blunt end down, on a work surface and cut off the kernels, running your knife down close to the cob. Add the kernels to the soup, return to the boil and simmer for 2–3 minutes. If using frozen corn, you will need about 500 g, simmered for the time recommended on the packet. Add the chicken, 1 teaspoon sesame oil and 2 teaspoons grated fresh ginger. Stir the slaked cornflour, taste and adjust the seasoning, then serve as in the main recipe. A beaten egg white can be whisked into the soup at the end.

japanese fresh corn soup
with spring onions and tamari soy sauce

A variation on a traditional Japanese summer soup, prized
for the fresh taste of corn – and very easy to make.

4 ears of fresh corn or about
500 g fresh corn kernels

1 litre hot First Dashi (page 17)
or Chicken Stock (page 14)

4 egg yolks

4 spring onions, sliced diagonally

2 tablespoons tamari (wheat-free soy)
or dark soy sauce

cracked pepper, or a Japanese pepper
mixture such as furikake seasoning or
seven-spice

serves 4

Bring a large saucepan of water to the boil, add the corn and simmer for about
2 minutes. Drain. Hold the corn upright on a chopping board, blunt end down.
Run a sharp knife down the cobs, shaving off the kernels. Reserve a few sliced-off
sections of kernels for serving, blanching them in boiling water for 2 minutes.

Put the remaining kernels in a blender with 250 ml stock. Purée until smooth, then
press through a strainer into a saucepan. Return the corn to the blender, add another
ladle of stock, purée, then strain as before, pushing through as much corn juice as
possible. Repeat until all the stock has been used. Reheat the mixture, then remove
from the heat.

Put 1 egg yolk into each of 4 small soup bowls, ladle the soup on top and beat with
chopsticks (the hot soup cooks the egg). Alternatively, whisk all 4 egg yolks in a mixing
bowl, beat into the soup, then ladle into bowls. Serve, topped with spring onions, the
reserved kernel sections, tamari or soy sauce and pepper to taste.

avgolemono
greek egg and lemon soup

250 ml long grain rice

1½ litres well-flavoured Chicken
(page 14) or Vegetable Stock (page 15)

2 eggs

grated zest and freshly squeezed juice
of 2 large unwaxed lemons

sea salt and freshly ground white pepper

a large handful of flat leaf parsley,
finely chopped

1 small lemon, finely sliced, to serve
(optional)

serves 4

I once lived in Melbourne, said to be the second biggest Greek city in the world, thanks to the large influx of Greek immigrants who arrived after the Second World War. It's a splendid place for Greek food, and I first tasted this classic Greek soup at lunch on a hot summer's day. It's incredibly fresh and easy to prepare. If you're serving it to guests, prepare the stock and rice first, then complete the dish just before serving.

Wash the rice well to remove the starch, then drain in a sieve.

Put the stock in a large saucepan and bring to the boil. Add the rinsed rice and return to the boil. Reduce to a simmer and cook for about 20 minutes or until the rice is tender. Season with salt and freshly ground white pepper.

Put the eggs in a small bowl and whisk well. Stir in the lemon juice and 1 tablespoon water.

Remove the soup from the heat and whisk one ladle of soup into the egg mixture. Add 2 more ladles, whisking again. Return the egg mixture to the pan and stir well.

Serve the soup in wide, shallow bowls, with a sprinkling of parsley and a little lemon zest. Float a few paper-thin slices of lemon on top if you like.

Note Do not reboil the soup after adding the eggs, or they will scramble.

pasta and noodles

pho bo
vietnamese beef noodle soup

2 packets fresh rice noodles or 4 bundles dried broad rice noodles or cellophane noodles (don't use egg or wheat-based ones)

1 onion, halved and thinly sliced

2–4 hot red chillies, deseeded if you like, but thinly sliced, plus extra to serve

250 g rump or fillet steak, very thinly sliced (freezing it first will make it easier to slice)

2 limes, quartered

4 handfuls of beansprouts, rinsed, drained and trimmed

a large bunch of coriander

a large bunch of Vietnamese basil (don't use ordinary basil – omit it if you can't find the real thing)

a large bunch of Vietnamese mint or ordinary mint

75 ml Asian fish sauce, to serve

easy vietnamese beef stock

1½ litres Beef Stock (page 12)

3–4 onions, finely sliced

3 cm fresh ginger, sliced

8 whole star anise

½ unwaxed lime or lemon, with skin, sliced

1 tablespoon Asian fish sauce

1 teaspoon sugar

serves 4

Pho bo, or beef soup, is probably the most famous dish to come out of Vietnam, one of the great classics. It is eaten mainly for breakfast, but you can find it almost any time of day. It is a wonderful combination of fresh herbs, full-flavoured stock, aromatic spices and deliciously filling noodles. *Pho* is pronounced 'far', and there are also chicken and vegetarian versions, though beef is best. If you were a pho vendor, you would take hours to make your stock, extracting every last nuance of flavour – this is a quicker version, because I love to make it at home. (The recipe for the real thing is on page 19.)

To make the Vietnamese beef stock, put all the stock ingredients in a saucepan, bring to the boil and simmer for 30 minutes. Keep hot.

Meanwhile, if using dried noodles, put them in a bowl and cover with hot water. Let soak for about 15 minutes, then drain and keep in cold water until ready to serve. If using fresh noodles, cut or separate them into strips, rinse in hot water for a few minutes, then keep in cold water until ready to serve.

Blanch the onion in boiling water for 2 minutes. Drain the noodles, dip in a saucepan of boiling water for a minute or so until hot, then divide between big soup bowls. Add the blanched onion and chillies, then put the sliced beef on top. Return the beef stock to the boil, then strain it into the bowls.

Lime wedges, beansprouts, a large quantity of herbs, extra chillies and extra fish sauce are all served separately.

Note In Vietnam, pho is not something people cook at home. Traditional home kitchens are small, and not set up for the long slow simmering of stock, which is always done in bulk. You go to pho vendors or pho restaurants, and if you ever go to Vietnam, ask the locals where the best ones are.

indonesian chicken noodle soup

1½ litres Chicken Stock
(page 14 or 19)

500 g chicken pieces, boneless
and skinless

1 carrot, finely sliced

2–3 tablespoons peanut oil

1 onion, finely sliced

1–2 bunches hon shigiri or enoki
mushrooms, root end removed and
mushrooms separated, or fresh
shiitakes, stems discarded,
caps halved

1 baby courgette, finely sliced
diagonally with a vegetable peeler

spice paste

2 stalks of lemongrass

2 tablespoons black pepper,
coarsely cracked

2 tablespoons fish sauce,
or 1 teaspoon shrimp paste (*belacan*)

2 teaspoons ground turmeric

8 pink Thai shallots or 2 small onions,
finely chopped

3 cm fresh ginger, peeled and grated

6 garlic cloves, crushed

a large handful blanched almonds
(about 125 ml)

to serve

rice ribbon or cellophane noodles,
fresh or dried

4 spring onions, finely sliced

2–4 green chillies, finely sliced

2 limes, cut into wedges

2 tablespoons pan-toasted peanuts,
coarsely chopped

serves 4

Use a whole chicken to make the stock from scratch, as in the recipe on page 19, or, as here, use ready-made stock and just poach the chicken pieces in it. Any number of vegetables may be added. I love Japanese mushrooms like enoki and hon shigiri, with their clumps of long stalks and little tea-cosy bonnets – all different sizes, all crowded together.

Bring the stock to the boil, add the chicken pieces, reduce the heat and poach gently until tender. Remove from the stock to a plate, let cool slightly, then shred into long pieces. Return the stock to the boil, add the carrots and simmer until tender. Remove the carrots and add to the chicken. Set the stock aside and keep it warm.

Meanwhile, if using dried noodles, put them in a bowl and cover with hot water. Let soak for about 15 minutes, then drain and keep in cold water until ready to serve. If using fresh noodles, cut or separate them into strips, soak in hot water for a few minutes, then keep in cold water until ready to serve.

To make the spice paste, cut the top off the lemongrass, keeping the white part only. Remove and discard the 2 outer leaves, and finely slice the rest. Put in a small blender or food processor, then add the pepper, fish sauce, turmeric, shallots, ginger, cloves and almonds and blend to a coarse paste. Alternatively, use a mortar and pestle. Set aside. You will use about 2 tablespoons for this recipe – freeze the rest in ice cube trays for future use.

Heat 2 tablespoons of the peanut oil in a wok, add the sliced onion and fry until crispy. Remove with a slotted spoon and drain on crumpled kitchen paper.

Reheat the oil, adding an extra tablespoon if necessary, then add the spice paste and fry gently until fragrant. Add the chicken and carrots, and stir-fry briefly to cover with the spices. Add the stock, mushrooms and courgette and heat until very hot – this will blanch the vegetables. Drain the noodles and divide between 4 noodle bowls. Ladle the chicken, vegetables and stock over the noodles and serve, topped with the spring onions, fried onions and half the chillies. Serve lime or lemon wedges, peanuts and remaining chillies in separate dishes.

grilled salmon noodle soup

Given some fresh salmon steaks and a kitchen stocked with some pretty basic Asian ingredients, this elegant dinner dish can be on the table in about 8 minutes – 30 if you're chatting and enjoying yourself over a glass of wine. Add whatever vegetables you have on hand. Tree ear mushrooms have no flavour, just an interesting texture and appearance, and a beautiful name.

1 tub silken tofu

2 bundles somen or soba noodles*

4 large salmon steaks, skin on

2 tablespoons sunflower oil

1 litre First Dashi (page 17) or dashi stock powder and water

your choice of other vegetables, such as sugar snap peas (a large handful per serving)

a handful of Chinese dried mushrooms, such as tree ear (optional), soaked in hot water for 20 minutes

about 6 spring onions, sliced

sea salt, fish sauce or soy sauce, to taste (optional)

freshly sliced chillies or chilli sauce (optional)

serves 4

If you prefer wheat-free noodles, you could substitute rice noodles or cellophane noodles (made from mung bean starch)

To prepare the tofu, put it between 2 plates and put a weight on top (a small can of tuna, for instance). This will force out some of the liquid and make it stick together better. Just before serving, cut into about 12 cubes – 3 cuts one way, 4 the other.

Bring a large saucepan of water to the boil and add the noodles. Have a glass of cold water ready. When the water comes to the boil, add a dash of cold water. When it returns to the boil, do it again, return to the boil and do it again. This will help cook the noodles perfectly right to the middle – the cold water 'frightens' the heat into the interior. Test after 3–4 minutes, then drain and keep in cold water until ready to serve.

Put the salmon in a plastic bag, add the oil and toss to coat. Bring a stove-top grill pan or frying pan to a high heat, then add the salmon, skin side down. When the skin is charred and the flesh has turned pale about 1 cm through, turn the salmon over and lightly sear the other side. It should stay pink except for a line on either side.

Bring the dashi to the boil, then lightly blanch your chosen vegetable. Remove with a slotted spoon. Drain the mushrooms and slice into pieces, discarding the hard stalk tip.

Put a pile of drained noodles into each bowl. Put the salmon steaks, skin side up, on top. Add the tofu cubes, mushrooms and any other vegetables used. Ladle the stock over the top and serve topped with spring onions. If you prefer, add seasoning in the form of salt, soy or fish sauce and fire in the form of fresh chillies or chilli sauce.

Variation Duck Noodle Soup

Instead of dashi, use any chicken stock. Instead of salmon, use 2–3 large duck breasts. Fry them skin side down over a low heat until the fat renders out – pour it off from time to time into a bowl and keep it to fry vegetables. When the fat has been rendered, about 20 minutes (you will see a line of crisp skin, then the flesh—the layer of fat will have disappeared), turn it over and cook at a high heat for about 5 minutes. It should be rare in the middle. Set aside for 5 minutes to set the juices. Just before serving, slice crosswise into thin slices and proceed as in the main recipe.

alphabet soup

Beloved of children everywhere, this baby soup pasta can be added to all sorts of other soups, but is especially useful with vegetable soups, to encourage the little beasts to eat their greens. I have included bacon because I love the flavour, and have used chicken stock, again for flavour. However, if you would like to stay vegetarian, use a well-flavoured vegetable stock and a few spoonfuls of crushed tomatoes, or just water.

Put the pancetta in a stockpot, heat gently and fry until the fat runs. Add the olive oil, heat briefly, then add the onion and cook gently until softened but not browned.

Add the potato, carrot, celery, courgettes, tomatoes and salt and pepper. Add the stock and the pasta and heat until simmering. Cook over low heat for about 15 minutes. Add the cabbage and beans, bring to the boil and cook for 5 minutes, then add the peas and canned beans and cook for another 2–3 minutes until all the vegetables are tender. Add salt and pepper to taste, sprinkle with parsley, then serve with bread and cheese (shown here melted on top of the bread).

Note A friend's children refuse to eat any soups with vegetable 'bits' in – if yours are like hers, cook the pasta and soup separately. Blend the soup element to a purée, then serve in bowls with a big spoonful of the pasta alphabets on top for them to stir in themselves.

100 g smoked pancetta, cut into cubes

1 tablespoon olive oil

½ onion, chopped

1 large potato, cubed and rinsed

1 carrot, quartered lengthways, then sliced crossways into triangles

2 celery stalks, sliced

2 small courgettes, quartered lengthways, then sliced crossways into triangles

3 tomatoes, halved, deseeded and chopped

1 litre Chicken Stock (page 14)

500 g alfabetto soup pasta

½ small round cabbage, quartered, cored and sliced

100 g green beans, cut into 2 cm lengths

100 g peas, fresh or frozen

about 200 g canned beans, such as cannellini, red kidney or chickpeas, about ½ small can, rinsed and drained

sea salt and freshly ground black pepper

to serve

2 tablespoons freshly chopped parsley

crusty Italian bread

a dish of freshly grated Cheddar cheese

serves 4

wonton chicken soup

8 Chinese cabbage leaves

1 cooked chicken breast, shredded

1 carrot, finely sliced lengthways, then blanched in boiling water for 1 minute

2 spring onions, finely sliced lengthways

a handful of fresh beansprouts, rinsed, drained and trimmed

wontons

125 g pork fillet or chicken breast, sliced

3 spring onions, chopped

a pinch of salt

1 teaspoon grated fresh ginger

2 canned water chestnuts, chopped

1 egg white, lightly beaten with a fork

12 small wonton wrappers

chinese chicken stock

1½ litres chicken stock

4 whole star anise

5 cm fresh ginger, peeled and sliced

1 onion, sliced

salt, to taste

serves 4

Most people might not realize that wontons are noodles. You can buy wonton wrappers or 'skins' either chilled or frozen in Chinese supermarkets. You peel off as many as you need, then the leftovers can be wrapped and kept frozen, ready for use at a moment's notice. Delicious wonton fillings take seconds to make in a food processor, and these little Chinese 'ravioli' can be used in soup, steamed and served with sauce, or even deep-fried and served as snacks. You can change the fillings too; pork, shrimp and other seafood are all wonderful.

Bring a large saucepan of water to the boil. Add the Chinese cabbage leaves and blanch for 1 minute. Plunge into a bowl of iced water for 5 minutes. Drain. Cut out and discard the white ribs. Put 4 leaves, one on top of the other, on a tea towel. Roll them up into a cylinder and press out the liquid. Cut the cylinder crossways into 3 cm long sections. Repeat with the other 4 leaves, to make little cabbage 'sushi'.

To make the wontons, put the sliced pork or chicken in a food processor and pulse until minced. Add the spring onions, salt and ginger and pulse again. Transfer to a bowl and stir in the water chestnuts. Brush a circle of egg white around the centre of each wonton wrapper and put 1 teaspoon of mixture in the middle. Twirl the wrapper around the filling to make a shuttlecock shape. Press to seal.

Put the stock ingredients in a saucepan and simmer for 10 minutes. Strain to remove the flavourings, then return the stock to the rinsed pan. Reheat the stock, add the wontons and poach them for 1½ minutes – they will rise to the surface like fresh pasta (which is what they are). Divide the wontons, stock, chicken, cabbage and carrot between heated soup plates, top with the spring onions and beansprouts and serve.

Note The cabbage rolls aren't a Chinese tradition, but Japanese. I was shown how to make them some years ago, and think they're a good way of including lots of leaves without them taking up too much room.

preparation of pasta, rice and noodles

Pasta and its Asian counterpart, the noodle, are perfect soup ingredients. The rules for cooking pasta are pretty simple, but those for cooking noodles vary, according to the materials from which they are made, and whether they're fresh or dried. Rice is used as a thickening agent, giving bulk and body to a soup.

pasta

Small soup pastas include children's favourites such as alfabetto, stelline (little stars) and rotelline (little wheels). Others include dozens of tiny versions of larger pasta, such as conchiglie (little shells) and ditalini. Some of the rice-shaped pasta is also good for soup – orzo and risoni for instance.

Add the pasta to the soup for the last 8–9 minutes of cooking (longer if the pasta is thick, hollow or ridged) or according to the directions on the packet.

rice

Rice absorbs double its volume of liquid and is perfect for providing body in soups. The grains of long grain and basmati rice will remain separate when cooked. Risotto and pudding rice become soft and sticky and lend their starches to the surrounding liquids.

noodles

The time that Asian noodles will take to cook depends on the starch or grain used to make them.

Cooking instructions are given for dried noodles, and also for fresh, when they are available in that form. The Japanese noodle cooking method (boxed text, right) deserves special mention – it is similar to the Spanish method of cooking fave beans.

wheat noodles

Wheat noodles are made from wheat flour either alone or in combination with some other starch (such as buckwheat in the case of soba noodles) or with egg. Wheat noodles are white, buckwheat noodles brown and egg noodles yellow. Wheat and egg noodles are available in various thicknesses, both dry and fresh.

Japanese Udon Noodles

Big, thick udon noodles are made in round, square or flat shapes. When using in soups, serve in dashi stock.

Fresh: rinse in warm water and boil for 1 minute
Dried: boil for 3–5 minutes (see boxed text)

Japanese Somen Noodles

In Japan, somen noodles are traditionally served cold with a dipping sauce, but are delicious in all kinds of noodle soups. Elegant, thin and white, they are often tied with ribbons in neat bundles.

Dried: boil for 3–4 minutes (see boxed text)

Japanese Ramen Egg Noodles

Pale yellow ramen noodles are based on Chinese egg noodles. Available fresh or dried.

Fresh: rinse in warm water and boil for 2 minutes
Dried: boil for 3–5 minutes (see boxed text)

Shanghai and Hokkien Noodles

White (wheat) or yellow (egg) Shanghai noodles and yellow (egg) Hokkien noodles are similar to Japanese ramen noodles, for which they can be substituted.

Fresh: rinse in warm water and boil for 2 minutes
Dried: boil for 3 minutes

Chinese Wheat Noodles

Often sold in 'nests' – one nest per serving.

Fresh: rinse in warm water, boil for 2–3 minutes
Dried: boil for 3–5 minutes

Chinese Thin Yellow Egg Noodles

Fresh: rinse in warm water, boil for 2 minutes
Dried: boil for 3–5 minutes

Chinese Thick Yellow Egg Noodles

Fresh: rinse in warm water, boil for 3 minutes
Dried: boil for 8 minutes

Chinese Wonton Wrappers or Skins

Made from wheat and egg noodle dough. Available fresh or frozen in packs of 175–225 g, usually 7.5 cm square.

Always fresh or frozen: sold in refrigerated section. If frozen, let thaw. If filling, add filling, seal, then boil for 1½–2 minutes until they rise to the surface, or deep-fry for 1 minute. These wrappers are sold in packs of 50–100 in various sizes. Leftover fresh wrappers may be resealed and frozen for future use (page 94).

rice noodles

Produced in south China and South-east Asia where rice rather than wheat is the main grain. Like pasta, they are made in many thicknesses from fine vermicelli to wide ribbons.

Fine Rice Vermicelli Noodles

Used in soups, salads and spring rolls.

Fresh: rinse in hot water, then cook for 1 minute
Dried: soak in hot water for 15 minutes and boil for 1 minute or deep-fry for 30 seconds

Thin Rice Vermicelli Noodles

Used in soups and spring rolls. Sold in large packets, or in small one-serving bundles of about 30 g each.

Fresh: rinse in hot water, then cook for 1 minute
Dried: boil for 1–2 minutes

Rice Ribbon Noodles

When fresh, often sold in folded sheets, like a small book. Sometimes uncut, so cut into wide strips before use. Can be used for Vietnamese pho noodle soups.

Fresh: rinse in hot water, then cook for 1 minute
Dried: soak in hot (not boiling) water for 15 minutes, then boil for 1 minute, or stir-fry for 1 minute. May also be deep-fried.

Rice Sticks

Available thick, medium and thin, all popular in soups. Wide ones are common in South-east Asian dishes. Fresh rice sticks are called rice sheet noodles and are sold in either pre-sliced or in whole sheet form.

Fresh: rinse in cold water, then cook for 1 minute
Dried: soak in hot (not boiling) water for 15 minutes, then boil for 1 minute, or stir-fry for 1 minute. May also be deep-fried.

Ricepaper Sheets

Dried translucent sheets of rice flour, round or triangular in shape. Used to make Vietnamese spring rolls. Rarely used for soup.

beanthread noodles

Made from mung bean flour, this family of almost translucent noodles is also known as cellophane or glass noodles, and include Japanese harusame noodles. They are most common in South-east Asia and well suited for people on low-carbohydrate or wheat-free diets. They are sold in various forms. Best, I think, are the packets of 30 g bundles, perfect for 1 serving.

Beanthread Noodles

Available in various thicknesses, excellent in soups.

Dried: soak in hot (not boiling) water for 15 minutes, then drain and boil or stir-fry for 1 minute

Japanese Harusame Noodles

Harusame means 'spring rain' and these noodles are thin, pale, delicate and semi-transparent and are mostly used in soups and salads. If unavailable, use shirataki noodles made from potato starch.

Fresh: rinse in fresh water and add direct to the dish
Dried: deep-fry until white and puffy – about 30 seconds

Japanese noodle cooking method

All dried Japanese noodles should be cooked in the same way. Bring a saucepan of water to the boil, add the noodles and return to the boil. Skim with a slotted spoon, then add a splash of cold water, return to the boil, then skim again. Repeat 2–3 times. When cooked, rinse to remove excess starch and reheat by dipping in boiling water. This is known as 'scaring the noodles'. A similar method is used to cook Spanish fava beans or fave (page 75).

---

buckwheat noodles

Usually made from a combination of buckwheat and wheat flour, and sometimes also yam potato starch.

Regular buckwheat noodles are a soft fawn colour. The green version, known as green tea noodles (cha-soba) contain ground green tea leaves. Buckwheat is not a wheat, though because these noodles contain a percentage of wheat flour they are not suitable for people on a wheat-free diet.

Japanese Soba Noodles

Usually made from a combination of buckwheat and wheat flour, and sometimes also yam potato starch.

A favourite in the Tokyo region, they are used in soup or served chilled with dipping sauce.

Fresh: boil for 2 minutes
Dried: boil for 4 minutes (see boxed text)

Korean Naeng Myun Noodles

Made from a mixture of buckwheat flour, potato starch and cornstarch, but not often used in soup.

Fresh: boil for 3 minutes
Dried: boil for 5 minutes

potato starch noodles

Made from yam potato starch (not related to regular potatoes), these noodles are not usually associated with soup dishes. However, they include Japanese fresh Shirataki Noodles and Korean dried Dang Myun Noodles.

big soups

bouillabaisse

People are very precious about bouillabaisse. Evidently, you can't make it anywhere except the Mediterranean. Tosh. The method is the same, wherever you live. Everywhere has its own typical fishes, and among them all you'll find enough different kinds to make a delicious dish. Make a large quantity – this is a dish for a sunny feast. If you're making it for a special occasion, add lobsters or crabs. The fish chunks will be mushed in a blender, so they can be any size, but a fisherman once told me that red fish have the best flavour. Gurnard, redfish and red snapper would all be good.

Rinse and dry all the fish. Put the clams or mussels, if using, in a large saucepan with 125 ml water, cover and heat until they open, shaking the pan from time to time. As they open, remove and set aside, discarding any that don't. Cook the crabs and lobsters separately, cleaning and breaking them into pieces to serve.

Heat the oil in a large flameproof casserole dish. Add the onion and leek, if using, and cook until softened and translucent. Add the tomatoes, garlic, bay leaves, thyme, orange zest, fennel, saffron and seasoning, then the fish fillets. Simmer for 10 minutes. Add the wine and boil hard for at least 10 minutes to drive off the raw flavour of alcohol. Add the water or stock, bring to a boil and boil hard for 15 minutes to amalgamate the water and oil. Ladle the solids into a mouli or food processor and work to a purée. Return the purée to the casserole dish and reheat.

Add the whole fish, bring to the boil, reduce the heat and simmer until the fish is opaque, about 2–3 minutes. Add the prawns and cooked clams or mussels, crabs and lobsters, if using, and simmer until the prawn tails turn red and the flesh opaque. Don't overcook or they will be tough and tasteless.

To make the rouille, put the bread in a bowl, wet with about 1 tablespoon water, then squeeze dry. Put the egg yolk, garlic, chillies and bread in a blender and purée until smooth. With the motor running, gradually add enough olive oil to make a thick paste.

Serve the fish and seafood on a large serving platter in the middle of the table. Strain the soup and ladle it into a tureen or soup plates and serve the toasted baguette and rouille separately. To eat, spread the slices of baguette with rouille, add to the soup and sprinkle with grated cheese. A two-course whole meal.

1 kg thick fish fillets, such as red snapper, cut into big chunks

1 kg whole fish, cleaned, scaled and gills removed

10–20 big clams and/or mussels (optional)

1–2 crabs and/or lobsters (optional)

125 ml extra virgin olive oil

1 onion, sliced

1 large leek, sliced (optional)

3 large tomatoes, skinned, deseeded and chopped

3 large garlic cloves, crushed

3 small fresh bay leaves

1 teaspoon dried thyme

1 strip of orange zest

1 slice of fennel

2 sachets Italian saffron powder

500 ml white wine

1 litre water or Fish Stock (page 14)

500 g shelled medium uncooked prawns, with tail fins intact

sea salt and freshly ground black pepper

rouille*

2 thick slices fresh French-style bread

1 egg yolk

3 garlic cloves, crushed

2 dried red chillies, deseeded and crushed

olive oil (see method)

to serve

baguettes, sliced diagonally and dried slightly in the oven

freshly grated cheese, such as Gruyère

serves 8–10

*There is an alternative recipe for rouille on page 120.

cioppino

1 kg fresh ripe red tomatoes
or 500 g canned Italian plum tomatoes

4 tablespoons olive oil

2 large onions, finely chopped

3 red peppers, peeled with a vegetable peeler, deseeded and chopped

6 garlic cloves, crushed with a pinch of salt

500 ml Fish Stock (page 14)

500 ml red wine, preferably Zinfandel

a large sprig of thyme

2 fresh bay leaves

1 teaspoon dried chilli flakes

500 g clams

500 g mussels, well scrubbed

12 shelled large uncooked prawns, with tail fins intact if possible

500 g scallops, halved through their thickness if very large

a large bunch of flat leaf parsley, chopped – keep the big stalks whole, bruise them a little and add to the stock (see method)

sea salt and freshly ground black pepper

to serve

a handful of basil
garlic bread

serves 4

All fishing communities seem to have their version of fish stew or soup, using trash fish they are unable to sell at the market. These fish are either strays, unpopular varieties or undersized. Cioppino is the creation of Italian fisherfolk in San Francisco and nowadays uses delicious shellfish – far from the trash fish of the past. It also includes Californian Zinfandel, though older recipes sometimes used white wine. Garlic bread, that darling of the old-fashioned dinner party, went seriously out of fashion for no good reason that I can see. It's Italian, it's American, it's perfect with Cioppino – and it tastes marvellous!

To prepare fresh tomatoes, cut a cross in the bottom, then put in a bowl of boiling water. Remove after 10–30 seconds and slip off the skins. Working over a sieve set over a bowl to catch the juices, cut the tomatoes in half and deseed into the sieve. Chop the tomatoes and set aside. Push the juices through the sieve with the back of a spoon – they taste terrific, but Italian food lore says that tomato seeds are bad for the liver, as well as getting stuck in the teeth. If using canned tomatoes, do the same.

Heat the oil in a large casserole over low heat. Add the onions and peppers and cook slowly for 5 minutes. Add the garlic and continue simmering until the onions have softened, about 15–20 minutes. If you cover the pot, the onions will soften quicker.

Add the fish stock, parsley stalks, wine, tomatoes and their juices, thyme, bay leaves and chilli flakes and bring to the boil over high heat. Reduce the heat and let simmer for about 30 minutes. The soup base can be held at this point until ready to serve. If you want to prepare in advance, cool and refrigerate until next day.

When ready to serve, put about 3 cm water in a large saucepan, add the clams and mussels, in batches if necessary, and bring to the boil with the lid on. Remove them as they open – try not to overcook, or they will be tough. Discard any shells that don't open. Strain the cooking liquid to remove any grit, then add to the soup base.

Bring the soup base to the boil, reduce the heat, add the prawns and scallops and cook for about 1 minute just until opaque. Add the reserved clams and mussels, let reheat for about 1 minute, season to taste, then stir in the chopped parsley. Serve in a tureen, or in soup bowls. Tear basil over the top and serve with garlic bread.

Note To serve more people, add about 1 kg firm white fish, such as snapper or cod, cut into large chunks, adding it before the prawns. Lobsters and crabs are also welcome additions – just clean them and cut into manageable pieces.

clam chowder

2 kg quahog clams, in the shell, or 1 kg smoked haddock

125 ml Fish Stock (page 14) or clam juice, plus extra fish stock to make 1 litre

500 g smoked pancetta, cut into cubes

sunflower oil (see method)

3 onions, coarsely chopped

1 celery stalk, chopped

1 carrot, chopped

2 bay leaves

a few sprigs of thyme

250 g salad potatoes, peeled and cut into cubes

500 ml double cream

sea salt and freshly cracked black pepper

a large bunch of flat leaf parsley, coarsely chopped

crackers, to serve

serves 4

There are many kinds of chowder – this New England variety, made with clams and cream, the Manhattan kind, made with tomatoes, and the British kind, made with corn and smoked haddock instead of the clams.

Put the clams in a large saucepan, then add 125 ml water and the fish stock or clam juice. Cover the pan, bring to the boil and boil hard until the clams open. Remove them as soon as they do and shell over a bowl. Don't overcook or they will be tough. Discard the shells, reserve the clams and return the juice in the bowl to the pan. Strain the cooking liquid through a sieve, then through muslin into a measuring jug. Add enough fish stock to make up to 1 litre. Taste it and reserve.

Clean the pan, add the bacon and cook slowly to render the fat (add a dash of oil to encourage it if you like – but sunflower, not olive). Remove the crisp bacon and set aside.

Add the onions, celery, carrots, bay leaves and thyme to the saucepan. Cook gently until the onions are softened and translucent. Add the potato cubes and the reserved 1 litre stock. Simmer until the potatoes are done, about 10 minutes.

Chop half the clams, and cut the others in half through their thickness. Add the clams, bacon and cream to the saucepan and heat through. Taste and add salt if necessary (remember the clam juices and bacon are already salty). Remove and discard the bay leaves and thyme.

Serve sprinkled with lots of cracked pepper, crisp bacon, handfuls of parsley and crackers.

Note To use smoked haddock, put the fish stock and water in a saucepan and bring to the boil. Add the haddock, reduce the heat to a bare simmer and leave until the fish can be flaked. Remove from the liquid and remove the skin from the fish. Discard the skin, put the fish on a plate a flake it into large chunks. Strain the stock.

Add 250 g frozen corn at the same time as the potatoes. Omit the crackers when serving.

laksa

Laksas are spicy soups from Malaysia, Indonesia and the Philippines, though the Malay ones are the best known. They contain vegetables, prawns, pork and noodles, though this varies from region to region. This one contains chicken, but do feel free to ring the changes with fish and other seafood instead. The spice paste is the key – usually laboriously made with a mortar and pestle, a blender is an easy, modern alternative.

Put all the spice paste ingredients into a spice grinder or blender and work to a paste (add a little water if necessary).

Heat the oil in a wok, add the spice paste and cook gently for about 5 minutes until aromatic. Add the thick part of the coconut milk (if any) and stir-fry until it throws out its oil, then add the thinner part and heat gently. Add 1 litre water and bring to the boil. Add the chicken, reduce the heat and poach gently without boiling until the chicken is cooked through, about 10–15 minutes. Add fish sauce or salt, to taste.

If using fresh noodles, rinse in cold water, then boil for about 1–2 minutes. If using dried noodles, cook in boiling unsalted water for 3–5 minutes, or until done, then drain. Divide the noodles between large soup bowls. Add the chicken and liquid, top with the beansprouts, spring onions, chilli and coriander, if using, and serve.

3 tablespoons peanut oil

500 ml canned coconut milk

2 boneless chicken breasts, skinned and thickly sliced

fish sauce or salt, to taste

750 g fresh or 100 g dried udon noodles

spice paste

3–6 red or orange chillies, cored and chopped

1 shallot, chopped

2 stalks of lemongrass, finely sliced

3 cm fresh ginger, finely sliced

½ teaspoon ground turmeric

6 blanched almonds, chopped

1 tablespoon fish sauce or a pinch of salt

1 garlic clove, crushed

to serve

1 packet fresh beansprouts, trimmed, rinsed and drained

4 spring onions, sliced diagonally

1 red chilli, cored and finely sliced

sprigs of fresh coriander (optional)

serves 4

hot and sour soup

Almost everyone in South-east Asia has a version of this soup. Interestingly it is the pineapple and tomatoes as well as the obvious tamarind that are seen as the sour part of the soup. Though this isn't one of the traditional versions, it's one I found in Hue, where I had an entire empty restaurant and half a dozen Vietnamese waiters to talk to. They had made the basic stock in the kitchen, then served it in a pan on a little tabletop burner. They added extra ingredients and served each one with some soup as it was ready. At home, you can cook everything together, with the fish and seafood added last, then serve it in bowls for people to add their own beansprouts and herbs.

Put the fish stock in a large saucepan, add the lemongrass, chillies, tamarind paste and/or pineapple, fish sauce and sugar. Bring to the boil and simmer for about 5 minutes. Add the tomatoes. Taste and adjust the seasoning with more fish sauce or sugar, as you like.

Add the fish and simmer for a few minutes until the flesh is opaque. Add the prawns and simmer until they are opaque and pink at the edges. Don't overcook or you will lose the flavour.

Put the beansprouts and spring onions into soup bowls, add the fish and prawns and handfuls of herbs. Ladle the broth over the top. Serve with little dishes of salt, pepper, kumquats, fish sauce with chillies and more herbs.

Variation As always in South-east Asia, noodles don't go astray. To make a more substantial meal, prepare your choice of rice noodles or cellophane noodles according to the directions on pages 96–7 and add to the bowls before the beansprouts.

1 litre Fish Stock (page 14) or water

3 fresh stalks of lemongrass, halved and crushed

2 red chillies, deseeded and halved

1 tablespoon tamarind paste and/or 2 slices small pineapple, cut into wedges

3 tablespoons fish sauce, plus extra to taste

1 tablespoon sugar, plus extra to taste

2 small tomatoes, preferably unripe, cut into wedges

about 500 g fish, such as small kingfish, huss or ribbonfish, cut crosswise into 4 cm steaks, or fillets

4–8 shelled medium uncooked prawns, with tail fins intact

a handful of beansprouts, trimmed, rinsed and drained

2 spring onions, chopped

to serve

4 large handfuls of Asian herbs, such as coriander, mint, sawtooth coriander, Asian basil (but not regular basil)

a small dish with 2 piles of salt and pepper

2 limes or a handful of kumquats, halved

a small dish of fish sauce

a small dish of chopped chillies

serves 4

chicken soup with vegetables

a handful of mini asparagus tips, halved crossways

a large handful of sugar snap peas, cut into 2–3 pieces each

1 punnet cherry tomatoes, quartered and deseeded

sea salt and freshly ground black pepper

southeast asian chicken stock

1 small organic chicken

2 whole star anise

2 cinnamon sticks

a handful of kaffir lime leaves

2 stalks of lemongrass, halved lengthways and bruised

3 inches ginger, peeled and sliced

4 garlic cloves, lightly crushed but whole

1 red chilli, halved lengthways

1 tablespoon peppercorns, bruised

to serve

1 chilli, red or green, sliced

coriander, Chinese chives, parsley, chives or other herbs

cooked noodles (optional)

serves 4

The basis of this soup is the simplest, best, most flavourful chicken soup in the world, an Asian stock even more wonderful than the legendary Jewish mother's chicken soup. The better the chicken, the better the stock, so invest in organic, kosher, free-range and all those desirable things.

Put all the chicken stock ingredients in a large saucepan, add water to cover the chicken by 3 cm, bring to the boil, reduce the heat and simmer for at least 1 hour.

Remove the chicken, whole, from the pan and reserve. Scoop out the solids from the stock, reserving the ginger. Put the ginger on a plate and cut into tiny slivers.

Strain the stock into a saucepan, ladling at first, then pouring through muslin. It should be clear but slightly fatty on top. The fat is not a problem for Asians, but Europeans may like to blot it off.

Taste the stock and reduce if necessary. Season to taste. Pull shreds of chicken off the bird and cut into bite-sized pieces if necessary. Put in a bowl and cover.

Return the stock to the boil, add the ginger slivers and thick parts of the asparagus and blanch for 30 seconds. Add the tips and blanch for 3 seconds more. Add the peas, tomato quarters and chicken and blanch for 30 seconds. You are heating them and keeping the peas and tomatoes fresh, rather than cooking them to a mush. Ladle into large soup bowls and top with sliced chilli and the herb of your choice. Noodles may also be added.

sausage soup

16 thin pork sausages, pricked with a fork

3 onions, chopped

3 tomatoes, skinned, deseeded and chopped

olive oil

250 g smoked pancetta or streaky bacon, coarsely chopped

2 garlic cloves, crushed with a pinch of salt

a large sprig of sage, sliced

1 baguette, sliced

250 g cheese, such as Cheddar, coarsely grated

sea salt and freshly ground black pepper

chopped parsley, to serve (optional)

serves 4

A deliciously simple soup from the south of France. I have an obliging butcher who will make all-meat sausages for me in 500 g batches. A revelation, and one of the best reasons for encouraging independent butchers and not buying meat from supermarkets. This serves four as a simple winter supper, but can be made more substantial by adding the suggestions in the note below.

Arrange the sausages in a ring around a large, shallow, flameproof casserole dish or baking dish, such as le Crueset. Put the onions and tomatoes in the middle and sprinkle with olive oil. Cook in a preheated oven at 200°C (400°F) Gas 6 until done (about 30 minutes, depending on the thickness of the sausages). Stir the onions and tomatoes after 15–20 minutes to stop them burning.

When the sausages are done, remove, cut into 3–4 pieces each and set aside. Put the dish on top of the stove and add the bacon. Fry, stirring, until crisp, and the fat is starting to run. Add the garlic and fry for about 1 minute, then add the sage. Add about 1 litre water and stir. Taste and adjust the seasoning, adding extra water if the mixture is too thick.

Meanwhile, put the slices of baguette on a baking tray and cook at the top of the oven until golden brown. Remove from the oven and sprinkle with grated cheese. Return to the oven until the cheese has melted and become almost crisp.

To serve, put about 3 cheese-topped croutes in 4 soup plates, ladle in the soup and top with the sausages. Sprinkle with parsley, if using, and serve.

Note If you like, serve the croutes separately. Adding them at the end keeps them crisp to the last possible moment, though the method of pouring the soup over them is very traditionally French.

The bacon may be omitted, but the soup will need more seasoning. Other vegetables such as quartered and sliced courgettes or cabbage may also be used.

goan chicken soup

Indians don't go in for soup – unless it's a remnant of some kind of colonial rule, as this one is. The Portuguese were so loath to give up their colonies when India gained independence in 1947 that it took another 20 years for them to be persuaded to leave Goa. Now, Christian Goa is the only place in India that you'll find beef and pork dishes, but chicken is acceptable to everyone except strict vegetarians. Somehow, Indian chickens just taste better than regular chickens, and there is no question that they are free range.

Heat the oil in a saucepan, add the onion, garlic and ginger and fry gently until softened but not browned. Add the rice, turmeric, salt and pepper and stock.

Simmer for 10 minutes, then add the peas and chicken and simmer until the rice is soft, about another 10 minutes.

To make the tempered topping (a favourite garnish in India), heat the oil in a wok or frying pan, add the mustard seeds and fry until they pop. Add the garlic and stir-fry until crisp. Take care, because it can easily burn and burnt garlic is bitter. Remove with a slotted spoon and set aside. Add the onions and stir-fry at a low temperature until well covered with oil. Continue cooking until tender. Add the curry leaves, if using, and cook for a few minutes until aromatic. Return the garlic to the mixture and remove from the heat.

To serve, ladle the soup into bowls, then top with the tempered mixture.

Note I like to use basmati rice in Indian dishes because it is so deliciously fragrant. However, it is the most prized and delicate of rice varieties, and should be handled gently because the grains can easily break.

1 tablespoon peanut oil or ghee

1 onion, finely chopped

3 garlic cloves, crushed

3 cm fresh ginger, peeled and grated

125 g rice, preferably basmati

½ teaspoon ground turmeric

1 litre Chicken Stock (page 14)

100 g shelled green peas

500 g cooked chicken, shredded into bite-sized pieces

sea salt and freshly ground black pepper

tempered topping

2 tablespoons peanut oil or ghee

1 tablespoon mustard seeds

2–4 garlic cloves, finely sliced crossways

3 small yellow onions, finely sliced

a handful of curry leaves (optional)

serves 4

duck soup

You can buy Thai curry pastes almost everywhere these days, but they're not hard to make yourself. If you would prefer to buy it, go to an Asian market where it will be closer to the real thing. I buy mine fresh in small tubs from a Thai shop, which also sells these typically Thai yellow egg-shaped aubergines, which are used for their bitter taste. Other colours won't be so bitter, but it's worth scooping out the middle seed section, which is the most bitter.

To make the curry paste, remove the seeds from the chillies if you like. Stir-fry the coriander and cumin seeds in a dry frying pan for 2 minutes to release the aromas. Let cool. Put all the paste ingredients in a spice grinder or blender and purée in bursts. Use 2–4 tablespoons for this recipe and freeze the remainder.

To prepare the duck breasts, preheat a wok, add 2 tablespoons of the peanut oil and sear the duck breasts on all sides. You are just sealing the outside – the inside should be raw. Remove, cool and freeze. Just before cooking, slice them very finely.

Soak the rice stick noodles, if using, in hot water for 15 minutes. Boil for 1–2 minutes, then drain and plunge into cold water.

Add the remaining peanut oil to the wok, add the aubergine pieces, if using, and stir-fry until browned on the edges and softened. Remove and set aside.

Add the 2–4 tablespoons curry paste to the wok and stir-fry gently to release the aromas. Add the sugar and stir-fry for a minute or so. Add 1 teaspoon of the fish sauce and stir-fry again. Add the stock and bring to the boil. Add the aubergines, if using, and the beans. Return to the boil and simmer for 15 minutes. Taste, add extra fish sauce as needed and set aside for 15 minutes.

When ready to serve, reheat the vegetables and stock, drain the noodles, cover with boiling water, then drain again.

Divide the noodles and vegetables between large bowls. Add the duck, ladle in boiling stock (which instantly cooks the duck), and serve with extra lime wedges and a dish of chopped chillies.

4 tablespoons peanut oil

1–2 skinless duck breasts

150 g dried wide rice stick noodles (optional)

3 egg-shaped yellow, white or purple aubergines, or small Chinese aubergines, quartered and deseeded (optional)

1 teaspoon sugar

2 tablespoons fish sauce, or to taste

1 litre South-east Asian Chicken Stock (page 19)

6 Chinese yard-long beans, sliced into 3 cm pieces, or 250 g green beans

thai red curry paste

5–10 dried red chillies, soaked in hot water for 30 minutes, then drained

½ teaspoon coriander seeds

½ teaspoon cumin seeds

1 garlic clove, crushed

2–3 pink Thai shallots or 1 regular chopped

3 cm fresh ginger or galangal, finely sliced

freshly grated zest of 1 lime, preferably a kaffir lime

1 tablespoon fish sauce

to serve

2–3 limes, cut into wedges

chopped chillies

serves 4

things on top

creamy things

Western-style soups are delicious with cream or creamy things on top. Stirred in, they give delicious richness to the base. Rouille and aïoli are traditional Provençal additions, while sour cream, crème fraîche and double or single cream are favourites everywhere.

aïoli – garlic mayonnaise

This garlic-laden mayonnaise is usually served as part of Le Grand Aïoli, the summer feast of vegetables, fish and seafood from Provence. It's

2 egg yolks, at room temperature

1 whole egg (if making in a food processor)

4 garlic cloves, crushed

a large pinch of salt

2 teaspoons freshly squeezed lemon juice or white wine vinegar

375 ml virgin olive oil

makes about 500 ml

If making in a food processor, put the egg yolks, whole egg, garlic, salt and lemon juice in the bowl and blend until pale. If making by hand, omit the whole egg. Gradually add the oil, a few drops at a time at first, then more quickly, but in stages, leaving a few seconds between additions to allow the eggs to 'digest' the oil. When all the oil has been added, if the mixture is too thick, add 1 tablespoon warm water. Serve immediately, or press clingfilm over the surface to prevent a skin from forming. It may be refrigerated for up to 3 days. In spring, when the garlic is milder, you can use more than later in the season.

rouille

This spicy sauce from Provence is one of the few French dishes which contains chilli. The romantic if notorious port of Marseilles was probably their point of entry – via North African or Portuguese traders.

125 g soft breadcrumbs

2–3 garlic cloves, peeled

2 dried red chillies, broken (shake out the seeds if you prefer a less spicy rouille)

3–4 tablespoons good olive oil

stock from bouillabaisse or water

makes about 200 ml

Put the bread in a bowl, sprinkle with 1 tablespoon water, press together, then squeeze out the water and put the wet bread in a blender. Add the garlic, chillies and olive oil and blend to a purée. Thin with 1–2 spoonfuls of fish stock from the soup (or water). Alternatively, use a mortar and pestle. Spread thickly on toast and float on top of the soup.

Variation You can also base rouille on regular mayonnaise. Omit the garlic from aïoli and use 2 teaspoons harissa paste, roasted mashed whole chillies or 1 tablespoon chilli paste.

crispy things

I don't know why, but the human palate just loves crispy, crunchy things. Yes, I know celery and apples fall into that category, but croutons, crisp fried bacon, cheese melted over thick, chunky toast all sound much more appetizing. Keep the celery and apples for the soup itself.

croutons

The traditional way to prepare croutons is to cut thick slices of bread, remove the crusts, then cut the remainder into cubes (day-old bread is best). Heat butter or butter and oil in a frying pan, add the cubes and sauté until golden on all sides. (I always find that it's too easy to burn them this way.)

Alternatively, put the cubes in a roasting tin, sprinkle with oil, toss to coat, then cook in a preheated oven at 200°C (400°F) Gas 6 until golden.

A friend of mine toasts the slices in a toaster until pale gold, then cuts into cubes and fries them in just a little butter and oil until golden.

I always find that my croutons squash into flat squares, not tidy cubes. So I prefer them more freeform, rough and ready. Tear good Italian bread into bits, heat some olive oil in a frying pan and sauté until golden on most sides. It is a little more rustic, but equally delicious. A garlic clove squashed into the oil makes them even better. However, if you prefer traditional, don't let me lead you astray.

toasted nuts and seeds

Almost any nut or seed will be improved by being lightly toasted in a dry frying pan before use. Think of pine nuts, and how amazingly good they taste after this treatment.

asian crispy things

Asian supermarkets sell interesting crispy things that are wonderful for topping all kinds of dishes. I like Vietnamese fried shallots, onions or garlic; Asian dried shrimp, which can be used as is, or ground to a powder and toasted some more; and Japanese bonito flakes, used in making dashi stock.

indian tempering

Indian cooks from many regions of the subcontinent have a delicious and interesting way of topping their curries, and I think it makes a delicious addition to regular soups.

Heat 1–2 tablespoons non-olive oil in a wok or small frying pan. Add 1 tablespoon mustard seeds (any kind). One or two other spices may be added at the same time – coriander seeds, fennel seeds or cumin, for instance. Fry until aromatic and the mustard seeds start bouncing out of the pan. Add other ingredients, such as a finely sliced small onion, sliced garlic or curry leaves, and fry until golden brown. Pour the mixture and its flavoured oil on top of the soup and serve.

vegetable crisps

Thinly slice onions, shallots, garlic, pumpkin or parsnips, using a mandoline or vegetable peeler. Fill a wok or deep-fryer one-third full of peanut oil or other mild oil (or to the manufacturer's recommended level).

Heat the oil to about 190°C (375°F) or to the manufacturer's recommended temperature. Test, using a sugar thermometer, or drop in a cube of bread – it should turn golden brown in 30–40 seconds.

Add the sliced vegetables in batches, not too many at a time, and cook on both sides until crisp and golden. Drain on crumpled kitchen paper. If you want to keep them warm, do so in a low oven.

eggs and cheese

poached eggs

Poached eggs added to a soup can turn it from a first course to a light lunch. Add the egg just before serving, because it is already cooked. Everyone seems to have their favourite way of poaching eggs – swirling whirlpools in the cooking water, or adding vinegar to the same water (but who wants an egg that tastes of vinegar!)

I was shown this one by an Australian food publisher, and it never fails. It keeps the white together because it's been very lightly cooked on the outside.

Bring water to the boil in a wide saucepan or frying pan. Put the eggs in a bowl and cover with hot water from the tap. Leave for 1 minute (or 10 seconds longer if you keep your eggs in the refrigerator). Don't leave it longer, or the white will stick to the inside of the shell. Pour off the water, then crack the eggs into a cup.

Turn the heat down so the water isn't boiling any more, then carefully slide the eggs separately into the pan. This way you don't get long strings of white flying all over the pan which you then have to discard. My friend would then put the lid on the pan for 4 minutes, though I keep it off so I can watch when they're ready. You want a set white and a soft yolk. I like to spoon the water over the top, too, so the yolk is nicely sealed.

Remove from the pan with a slotted spoon and transfer to a bowl of cold water. Leave them there until you're ready to serve. Using the slotted spoon, remove them from the water, then blot the bottom of the spoon with kitchen paper, add the egg to the hot soup and serve immediately.

cheese

Is there anyone in the world who can resist adding a spoonful or so of grated or shaved Parmesan to a soup?

But a word of warning – don't add them to the soup when it's still boiling hot, or they will seize into a nasty lump.

If you're using Parmesan, PLEASE use it freshly grated from the block. Use the large side of a box grater to grate Cheddar. It's softer, so won't grate as finely. This is one of my favourite varieties for melting on top of toast to make a cheesy croute (page 113).

herbs

Some herbs are cooked in the soup, then removed before eating – bay leaves, whole stalks of lemongrass, lime leaves and rosemary for example. Others may be used as a topping, in various forms.

fresh herbs

The ubiquitous sprig is the bane of my life. My rule is, if you can't eat it, don't serve it. If you can't fit it on your spoon, don't serve it. So, if your heart is set on a sprig, make sure it's a little one – just the pinched-out end of a sprig.

Whole leaves look and taste good, while the flavour of some herbs benefits from a bit of GBH. Parsley is forever being chopped – just do it coarsely, because if you chop it finely you lose all its flavour. If you're using basil, remember never cut or chop it, always tear it. Then you don't get black, damaged edges.

If you're using chives, cut them with kitchen scissors, otherwise you get crushed, darkened surfaces. I like parsley to be scissor-snipped, too.

crisp-fried herbs

Herb leaves such as parsley, sage, curry leaves and others are delicious fried to a crisp, either in a wok or deep-fryer as above, or shallow-fried in a frying pan using olive oil or a mixture of butter and oil. Remove and drain on kitchen paper.

basil or parsley oil

You can buy herb oils and chilli oils, but I much prefer to make them myself. To make basil oil, put a large handful of basil in a food processor and add at least 250 ml olive oil. Blend, set aside for 30 minutes or overnight in the refrigerator, then strain into a clean bottle. Other herbs, such as parsley, may be used instead. The result is a bright green, assertively flavoured oil – trail it sparingly over the surface of the soup when serving.

pesto

Although in Italy, pesto is served only with pasta, the rest of the world has fallen in love with it. It makes a delicious dressing for many kinds of salad – potato, tomato, chickpeas and beans – or stirred through rice or couscous with extra herbs.

basil pesto

4 tablespoons pine nuts
4 garlic cloves, crushed
1 teaspoon sea salt
a large double handful of basil leaves
25 g freshly grated Parmesan cheese
125 ml extra virgin olive oil, or to taste
makes about 250 ml

Put the pine nuts in a dry frying pan and fry gently and quickly until golden (about 30 seconds). They burn very easily, so don't leave them. Let cool. Transfer to a food processor or blender, add the garlic, salt and basil and purée to a paste. Add the Parmesan, blend again, then add the oil and blend again until smooth. Add extra oil if you want a looser texture.

salt, fire, sour

These three tastes, together with sweet sugar, are the cornerstones of South-east Asian cooking, but they are happy in any kind of cuisine.

salt

Salt can be added in various forms, not just as regular salt.

pancetta and bacon

There's nothing more delicious than salty, smoky ham or bacon, fried until crisp, then added to soup. I like cubed unsmoked pancetta, streaky bacon, bacon lardons, thinly sliced smoked pancetta, or Italian Parma ham in any guise.

It's better to use fatty kinds of bacon such as streaky or Italian pancetta, because as the fat renders out it leaves a crisper result behind. I like the smoked kind and ask the shopkeeper to cut it as fine as paper, so it will be super-crisp when cooked. Even supermarkets now sell little square tubs of cubetti – pancetta cut into squares.

anchovies

Anchovies act much as soy or fish sauce do in Asian cooking – as a salt flavour, but a more interesting, smoky kind of salt. Use them as fillets, or mash them into soffrito at the beginning of the soup.

soy sauce

There are many kinds of soy sauce available. In Chinese cooking, the most common are light and dark. Though light sounds better, it is in fact the saltier of the two. In Japanese cooking, there are a number of different kinds. If you are trying to avoid wheat, Japanese tamari sauce is the only one that doesn't contain wheat.

fish sauce

This is South-east Asia's version of soy sauce. I prefer it to soy, because its flavour is more subtle. Those most widely available in the west are Thai *nam pla* and Vietnamese *nuòc mam*, though there is also *patis* from the Philippines and *shottsuru* from Japan.

fire

chillies

You either love them or hate them. If you're making Asian soups, serve most of the chillies separately, for people to add their own. A true chilli-head will like them with the hot seeds included. The rule for pointed chillies is – the smaller they are the hotter they are. Equally hot are the big, fat Caribbean chillies such as Scotch bonnet and habaneros.

To prepare chillies, halve and deseed them, and scrape out the membrane, which is the hottest thing of all.

Some cuisines, especially Mexican, for some dishes grill them like peppers to remove the skin and add a smoky sweet flavour.

Some people wear latex gloves to handle them, but unless you're doing hundreds, why bother? To remove chilli, onion and other smells from your hands, there is a metal 'egg' available in kitchen shops designed to remove garlic smells. I find it works with chilli, too – not completely, though, so don't touch your face if you've been handling chillies. I've also tried rinsing my fingers in milk or yoghurt, which is a time-honoured idea from India. It doesn't remove all of it, but it helps.

chilli oil

To make chilli oil, put a few fresh or dried chillies in a small bottle of oil. Let steep for a few hours or up to 1 day, then taste. If the oil is spicy enough for you, strain out the chillies, return the oil to the bottle and seal. If not, let steep longer, to taste.

pepper

Never use ready-ground pepper. It loses its flavour and pungency soon after grinding, so buy whole peppercorns and grind them yourself to a texture that suits you. If you want cracked pepper rather than ground, use a mortar and pestle or put between 2 sheets of paper and roll with a rolling pin. Chinese dishes usually call for white pepper, Italian for black. Other varieties include dried green pepper, dried red pepper (not a true pepper) and the spicy, lip-numbing Chinese Szechuan pepper.

sour

lemon zest and lime zest

An unbeatable addition to all sorts of foods. Think of lime added to tropical flavours and lemon to more temperate ones. Remove the zest in shreds or grate it finely. Whatever you use, invest in a good zester, one that doesn't include the bitter white pith. Even more important is to choose unwaxed fruit, or to wash off the wax with warm water (if it's too hot, it will release the essential oils and you'll lose some of the flavour).

limes, lemons and kumquats

In South-east Asia, many soups are served with lime wedges so you can add a squeeze of juice to suit yourself.

When I was in Vietnam, I was delighted to find a real use for kumquats, which were used just like limes, and tasted perfect. Previously, I'd only ever preserved them in brandy and sugar, pouring off the liquid as a homemade liqueur.

websites and mail order

Food Suppliers

Selfridges Food Hall
Selfridges, 400 Oxford Street,
London W1A 1AB
Tel: 020 7318 3899
Mail order available.

Organic Food

The Fresh Food Company
Tel: 020 8749 8778
www.freshfood.co.uk
*Weekly box delivery nationwide:
meat, fish, vegetables, fruit, bread,
wine, beer.*

Graig Farm Organics
Tel: 01597 851655
www.graigfarm.co.uk
*Organic fish, dairy produce,
groceries, fruit, vegetables and
organic alcohol.*

Organics Direct
Tel: 01604 791911
www.organicsdirect.co.uk
*Home delivery of organic food
boxes.*

West Country Organics
West Country Organics Ltd,
Natson Farm, Tedburn St Mary,
Exeter, Devon EX6 6ET
Tel: 01647 24724
www.westcountryorganics.co.uk
*Delivers food boxes weekly
nationwide, including salads and
herbs.*

Herbs, Spices and Oils

Cool Chile Company
PO Box 5702, London W11 2GS
Tel: 0870 902 1145
www.coolchile.co.uk
*Dried chillies and Mexican
ingredients.*

Extra Virgin Olive Oils and Mediterranean Foods
Tel: 01460 72931
www.getoily.com
*Olive oils and Mediterranean
produce.*

Fox's Spices
Fox's Spices, Dept GF,
Masons Rd,
Stratford upon Avon CV37 9NF
Tel: 01789 266 420
*Mail order catalogue for herbs,
spices.*

Peppers by Post
Sea Spring Farm, West Bexington,
Dorchester, Dorset DT2 9DD
Tel: 01308 897892
Email:
michael@csespringphotos.com
*Mail order for fresh, home-grown
chillies in season (July–December).*

The Spice Shop
Tel: 0207 221 4448
www.thespiceshop.co.uk
Fresh spices, blends and herbs.

Fish

The Fish Society
Tel: 0800 074 6859
www.thefishsociety.co.uk
*Fresh fish including organic and
wild salmon, smoked fish and
shellfish. Next day delivery.*

Seafooddirect
Tel: 08000 851549
www.seafooddirect.co.uk
Home delivery of fish and seafood.

Wing of St Mawes
Tel: 0800 052 3717
www.cornish-seafood.co.uk
*Fresh and smoked fish. Next day
delivery.*

Poultry and Meat

The Country Butcher
Tel: 01452 831585
www.countrybutcher.co.uk
*Award-winning sausages,
traditional bacon.*

Providence Farm Organic Meats
Tel: 01409 254421
www.providencefarm.co.uk
*Organic pork, beef, chicken and
duck.*

Scottish Organic Meats
Tel: 01899 221747
www.scottishorganicmeats.com
Organic beef, lamb, pork, chicken.

Asian Food Suppliers

Sri Thai (Thai)
56 Shepherd's Bush Road,
London W6 7PH
Tel: 020 7602 0621

Super Bahar
(Iranian and Middle Eastern)
349 Kensington High Street,
London W8 6NW
Tel: 020 7603 5083

Talad Thai (Thai, South-east Asian)
320 Upper Richmond Road,
London SW15 6TL
Tel: 020 8789 8084

Tawana Oriental Supermarket (Thai)
18 Chepstow Road,
London W2 5BD
Tel: 020 7221 6316

Thanh Xuân Supermarket (Vietnamese)
84 Deptford High Street,
London SE8 4RG
Tel: 020 8691 8106

TK Trading (Japanese)
Unit 7, The Chase Centre, Chase
Road, North Acton, London
NW10 6QD
Tel: 020 8453 1743/1001
www.japan-foods.co.uk (in
Japanese)
Email: tktrade@uk2.so-net.com

Asian Specialist Food districts

Southall, Tooting and Wembley
Three areas full of Indian,
Bangladeshi and Pakistani
grocers and shops, stocking a
wide range of South Asian spices
and ingredients.

Edgware Road, London
Lebanese and Middle Eastern
spices and ingredients.

Gerrard Street area, Soho, London
Chinese, Japanese, South-east
Asian.

index